BECAUSE OF
Bethlehem

Also by Max Lucado

Inspirational

3:16
A Gentle Thunder
A Love Worth Giving
And the Angels Were Silent
Before Amen
Come Thirsty
Cure for the Common Life
Facing Your Giants
Fearless
Glory Days
God Came Near
Grace
Great Day Every Day
He Chose the Nails
He Still Moves Stones
In the Eye of the Storm
In the Grip of Grace
It's Not About Me
Just Like Jesus
Max on Life
More to Your Story
Next Door Savior
No Wonder They Call Him the Savior
On the Anvil
Outlive Your Life
Six Hours One Friday
The Applause of Heaven
The Great House of God
Traveling Light
When Christ Comes
When God Whispers Your Name
You'll Get Through This

Fiction

Christmas Stories
The Christmas Candle
Miracle at the Higher Grounds Café

Bibles (General Editor)

Grace for the Moment Daily Bible
The Lucado Life Lessons Study Bible
Children's Daily Devotional Bible

Children's Books

A Max Lucado Children's Treasury
Do You Know I Love You, God?
God Forgives Me, and I Forgive You
God Listens When I Pray
Grace for the Moment: 365
Devotions for Kids
Hermie, a Common Caterpillar
Itsy Bitsy Christmas
Just in Case You Ever Wonder
Lucado Treasury of Bedtime Prayers
One Hand, Two Hands
Thank You, God, for Blessing Me
Thank You, God, for Loving Me
The Boy and the Ocean
The Crippled Lamb
The Oak Inside the Acorn
The Tallest of Smalls
You Are Mine
You Are Special

Young Adult Books

3:16
It's Not About Me
Make Every Day Count
Wild Grace
You Were Made to Make a Difference

Gift Books

Fear Not Promise Book
For the Tough Times
God Thinks You're Wonderful
Grace for the Moment
Grace Happens Here
His Name Is Jesus
Let the Journey Begin
Live Loved
Mocha with Max
Safe in the Shepherd's Arms
This Is Love
You Changed My Life

BECAUSE OF

Bethlehem

LOVE IS BORN, HOPE IS HERE

MAX LUCADO

THOMAS NELSON
Since 1798

Published in Nashville, Tennessee, by Thomas Nelson. Thomas Nelson is a registered trademark of HarperCollins Christian Publishing, Inc.

Thomas Nelson titles may be purchased in bulk for educational, business, fund-raising, or sales promotional use. For information, please e-mail SpecialMarkets@ThomasNelson.com.

Unless otherwise noted, Scripture quotations are taken from the Holy Bible, New International Version®, NIV®. Copyright © 1973, 1978, 1984, 2011 by Biblica, Inc.® Used by permission of Zondervan. All rights reserved worldwide. www.zondervan.com. The "NIV" and "New International Version" are trademarks registered in the United States Patent and Trademark Office by Biblica, Inc.®

Scripture quotations marked GNT are from the Good News Translation in Today's English Version—Second Edition. Copyright 1992 by American Bible Society. Used by permission. Scripture quotations marked THE MESSAGE are from The Message. Copyright © by Eugene H. Peterson 1993, 1994, 1995, 1996, 2000, 2001, 2002. Used by permission of Tyndale House Publishers, Inc. Scripture quotations marked NASB are from New American Standard Bible®. Copyright © 1960, 1962, 1963, 1968, 1971, 1972, 1973, 1975, 1977, 1995 by The Lockman Foundation. Used by permission. (www.Lockman.org). Scripture quotations marked NCV are from the New Century Version®. © 1987, 1988, 1991 by Word Publishing, a division of Thomas Nelson, Inc. Used by permission. All rights reserved. Scripture quotations marked NET are from the NET Bible®. Copyright © 1996–2006 by Biblical Studies Press, L.L.C. http://netbible.com. All rights reserved. Scripture quotations marked NIrV are from the Holy Bible, New International Reader's Version®, NIrV®. Copyright ©1995, 1996, 1998, 2014 by Biblica, Inc.® Used by permission of Zondervan. All rights reserved worldwide. www.zondervan.com. The "NIrV" and "New International Reader's Version" are trademarks registered in the United States Patent and Trademark Office by Biblica, Inc.® Scripture quotations marked NKJV are from the New King James Version®. © 1982 by Thomas Nelson. Used by permission. All rights reserved. Scripture quotations marked NLT are from the Holy Bible, New Living Translation. © 1996, 2004, 2007, 2013 by Tyndale House Foundation. Used by permission of Tyndale House Publishers, Inc., Carol Stream, Illinois 60188. All rights reserved. Scripture quotations marked NRSV are from New Revised Standard Version Bible. Copyright © 1989 National Council of the Churches of Christ in the United States of America. Used by permission. All rights reserved. Scripture quotations marked RSV are from Revised Standard Version of the Bible. Copyright 1946, 1952, and 1971 National Council of the Churches of Christ in the United States of America. Used by permission. All rights reserved. Scripture quotations marked TLB are from The Living Bible. Copyright © 1971. Used by permission of Tyndale House Publishers, Inc., Carol Stream, Illinois 60188. All rights reserved. Scripture quotations marked THE VOICE are from The Voice™. © 2012 by Ecclesia Bible Society. Used by permission. All rights reserved. Note: Italics in quotations from The Voice are used to "indicate words not directly tied to the dynamic translation of the original language" but that "bring out the nuance of the original, assist in completing ideas, and . . . provide readers with information that would have been obvious to the original audience" (The Voice, preface). Scripture quotations marked WEB are from the World English Bible™. Public domain.

All hymns are taken from the public domain unless otherwise noted.

ISBN: 978-0-8499-4759-9
ISBN: 978-0-7180-8600-8 (IE)
ISBN: 978-0-7180-9131-6 (Autographed Edition)
ISBN: 978-0-7180-9129-3 (Custom)

Library of Congress Control Number: 2016939084

Printed in the United States of America
16 17 18 19 20 [RRD] 6 5 4 3 2 1

*Denalyn and I are honored to dedicate this book
to Randy and Rozanne Frazee.
Able workers.
Devoted servants.
Wonderful friends.*

Contents

Acknowledgments

*W*ise men, shepherds, and angels. They came to Joseph and Mary. They came to me as well. Thanks to the following folks, this book was completed.

Editors Liz Heaney and Karen Hill—Such diligence and patience.

Copy editor Carol Bartley—No error slips past your skillful eyes.

The management team of Steve and Cheryl Green—Truer friends cannot be found.

The TN publishing group led by Mark Schoenwald, David Moberg, LeeEric Fesko, and Liz Johnson—I sincerely appreciate your untiring support.

Consultants and publicists Greg and Susan Ligon and Jana Muntsinger—Every author should have your creative assistance.

Prayer warrior David Treat—Ever present, ever interceding. Just like Jesus.

The Oak Hills Church—Each time I step into the pulpit, I think, *Are they not tired of me yet?* But you keep showing up.

Administrative assistants Janie Padilla and Margaret Mechinus—Hour by hour solving problems, offering support. So valuable.

My family: Brett, Jenna, Andrea, Jeff, and Sara—You make this papa's heart burst with pride.

Grandbaby Rose—Your mom delivered you into the world at the time I delivered this book to be published. Your arrival is the one that matters! Welcome!

And dear, dear Denalyn—Because of you I've enjoyed Christmas every day for thirty-four years. Love you.

1

I Love Christmas

I love Christmas. Let the sleigh bells ring. Let the carolers sing. The more Santas the merrier. The more trees the better.

I love Christmas. The ho ho ho, the rooty toot toot, the thumpety, thump, thump, and the pa rum pa pum pum. The "Silent Night" and the sugarplums.

I don't complain about the crowded shops. I don't grumble at the jam-packed grocery store. The flight is full? The restaurant is packed? Well, it's Christmas.

And I love Christmas.

Bring on Scrooge, Cousin Eddie, and the "official Red Ryder, carbine-action, two-hundred shot range model air rifle." "You'll shoot your eye out!"

The tinsel and the clatter and waking up "to see what was the matter." Bing and his tunes. Macy's balloons. Mistletoe kisses, Santa Claus wishes, and favorite dishes. Holiday snows, warm winter clothes, and Rudolph's red nose.

I love Christmas.

I love it because somewhere someone will ask the

Christmas questions: What's the big deal about the baby in the manger? Who was he? What does his birth have to do with me? The questioner may be a child looking at a front-yard crèche. He may be a soldier stationed far from home. She may be a young mom who, for the first time, holds a child on Christmas Eve. The Christmas season prompts questions.

> I love Christmas because somewhere someone will ask the Christmas questions: What's the big deal about the baby in the manger?

I can remember the first time I asked those questions. I grew up in a small West Texas town, the son of a mechanic and a nurse. Never poor but certainly not affluent. My dad laid pipeline in the oil fields. Mom worked the three-to-eleven shift at the hospital. I followed my brother to elementary school every morning and played neighborhood ball in the afternoons.

Dad was in charge of dinner. My brother washed the dishes, and I was in charge of sweeping the floor. We boys took our baths by eight and were in bed by nine with permission to do one thing before turning out the lights. We could read.

The chest at the foot of our bed contained children's books. Big books, each with a glossy finish and bright pictures. The three bears lived in the chest. So did the big, bad wolf and seven dwarfs and a monkey with a lunch pail, whose name I don't recall. Somewhere in the chest, beneath the fairy tales, was a book about baby Jesus.

On the cover was a yellow-hayed manger. A star glowed above the stable. Joseph and a donkey, equally big eyed, stood nearby. Mary held a baby in her arms. She looked down at him, and he looked up at her, and I remember looking at them both.

My dad, a man of few words, had told my brother and me, "Boys, Christmas is about Christ."

In one of those bedtime, book-time moments, somewhere between the fairy tales and the monkey with the lunch pail, I thought about what he had said. I began asking the Christmas questions. In one way or another, I've been asking them ever since.

I love the answers I have found.

Like this one: God knows what it is like to be a human. When I talk to him about deadlines or long lines or tough times, he understands. He's been there. He's been *here*. Because of Bethlehem, I have a friend in heaven.

Because of Bethlehem, I have a Savior in heaven. Christmas begins what Easter celebrates. The child in the cradle became the King on the cross. And because he did, there are no marks on my record. Just grace. His offer has no fine print.

He didn't tell me, "Clean up before you come in." He offered, "Come in and I'll clean you up." It's not my grip on him that matters but his grip on me. And his grip is sure.

Because of Bethlehem, I have a Savior in heaven. Christmas begins what Easter celebrates. The child in the cradle became the King on the cross.

So is his presence in my life. Christmas presents from Santa? That's nice. But the perpetual presence of Christ? That's life changing.

God is always near us. Always for us. Always in us. We may forget him, but God will never forget us. We are forever on his mind and in his plans. He called himself "'Immanuel' (which means 'God with us')" (Matt. 1:23).

Not just "God made us."

Not just "God thinks of us."

Not just "God above us."

But God *with* us. God where we are: at the office, in the kitchen, on the plane. He breathed our air and walked this earth. God . . . with . . . us!

We need this message more than ever. We live in anxious times. Terrorism is living up to its name—terror. Violence hangs over our planet like a dark cloud. Think about the images on the news: the senseless attacks, the bloodshed, the random acts of cruelty.

And, as if the malice were inadequate, there is the fear of another recession. We seem to teeter on the edge of bull markets going bear and the financial world going down. The shepherds stayed awake, watching their flocks by night. You've been sleeping with one eye open trying to keep watch over your stocks by night.

And there is more:

The job you can't keep
The tumor you can't diagnose
The marriage you can't fix
The boss you can't please

We can relate to the little boy who played the part of the angel in the Christmas story. He and his mother rehearsed his lines over and over: "It is I; don't be afraid." "It is I; don't be afraid."

Yet, when the Christmas pageant began, he walked onto the stage and saw the lights and audience and he froze. After an awkward silence, he finally said, "It is me and I'm scared."

Are you scared? If so, may I suggest that you need a little Christmas? I don't mean a dose of saccharine sentiment or Santa cheer or double-spiked eggnog. That's not Christmas.

Christmas, as my dad said, is about Christ. Christ's name occupies six of the nine letters, for crying out loud. This isn't Santa-mas, or shopping-mas, or reindeer-mas. This is *Christ*-mas. And *Christ*-mas is not *Christ*-mas unless or until you receive the message of Bethlehem.

God is always near us. Always for us. Always in us. We may forget him, but God will never forget us.

Have you? In the hurry and scurry of the season, have you taken time to receive the promise of the season?

- God gets us.
- God saves us.

God is always near us. By the way, Bethlehem was just the beginning. Jesus has promised a repeat performance. Bethlehem, Act 2. No silent night this time, however. The skies will open, trumpets will blast, and a new kingdom will begin. He will empty the tombs and melt the winter of death. He will press his thumb against the collective cheek of his children and wipe away all tears. "Begone, sorrow, sickness, wheelchairs, and cancer! Enough of you, screams of fear and nights of horror! Death, you die! Life, you reign!" The manger invites, even dares us to believe the best is yet to be. And it could all begin today.

But if it doesn't, there is a reason. No day is accidental or incidental. No acts are random or wasted. Look at the Bethlehem birth. A king ordered a census. Joseph was forced to travel. Mary, as round as a ladybug, bounced on a donkey's back. The hotel was full. The hour was late. The event was one big hassle. Yet, out of the hassle, hope was born.

It still is. I don't like hassles. But I love Christmas because it reminds us how "God causes everything to work together for the good of those who love God" (Rom. 8:28 NLT).

The heart-shaping promises of Christmas. Long after the guests have left and the carolers have gone home and the lights have come down, these promises endure.

Perhaps you could use some Christmas this Christmas?

Let's do what I did as a six-year-old, redheaded, flat-topped, freckle-faced boy. Let's turn on the lamp, curl up in a comfortable spot, and look into the odd, wonderful story of Bethlehem.

May you find what I have found: a lifetime of hope.

2

God Has a Face

*W*hy do we punch elevator buttons more than once?

Why do we love the front seat of a bus and the backseat of a church?

Why do we pierce holes in our bodies and hang jewelry from them?

Why do we ask for instructions and then argue with the person who gave them?

Of what purpose is a necktie?

Rational behavior is not one of our trademarks. But if you want to see people on the edge of insanity, just watch the way families treat their babies at Christmastime.

The poor child has no warning. He is just starting to recover from the slide down the birth canal when the family begins decorating him as if he were a puppy in the dog parade. Red furry stocking cap with a white ball on the end. Goofy elfish shoes that curl at the toes. When this baby becomes a teen and wears baggy jeans and sports a tattoo, grown-ups will groan at the sight. But dress a six-month-old in suspenders and reindeer antlers? That's cute.

And the gifts we give. The little one can't get out of her crib, yet ever-earnest Mommy has her hooked on phonics. He can't even walk without help, and Grandpa gives him a Louisville Slugger baseball bat.

And the pictures we take!

Baby teething on the ornaments
Baby snoozing under the tree
Baby on Santa's lap
Santa with wet spot on lap

We make such a fuss! Bring the baby into a room, and everything changes. Grandma reaches up. Grandpa wakes up. Conversation shifts from politics and presidents to Pampers and pacifiers. This time of year babies take center stage. And well they should. Is not Christmas the story of a baby?

Heaven's seed enwombed in Mary.
Minuscule, yet mighty.
A fetus, yet a force.
God descends a birth canal.
Born.
Creator cradled in a Bethlehem barn.
Infant, yet infinite.
Asleep, yet a King.

God gurgles in Mama's arms.

Baby.

This is the Christmas moment that shaped all the others to follow. On a starlit night in the company of sheep, cattle, and a bewildered Joseph, Mary's eyes fell upon the face of her just-born son. She was bone weary, surely. In pain, likely. Ready to place her head on the straw and sleep the rest of the night away, probably. But first Mary had to see this face. *His* face. To wipe the moisture from his mouth and feel the shape of his chin. To be the first to whisper, "So this is what God looks like."

Jesus entered our world not *like*
a human but *as* a human.

People have always wondered about the image of God. Societies have speculated. Tribes have cogitated. And we've reached a variety of conclusions. God has been depicted as a golden calf and a violent wind and an angry volcano. He wears wings, breathes fire, eats infants, and demands penance. We've fancied God as ferocious, magical, fickle, and maniacal. A god to be avoided, dreaded, and appeased. But never in mankind's wildest imaginings did we consider that God would enter the world as an infant.

"The Word became flesh and dwelt among us" (John 1:14 NKJV). The Word became not a whirlwind or a devouring fire but a single cell, a fertilized egg, an embryo—a baby. Placenta nourished him. An amniotic sac surrounded him. He grew to the size of a fist. His tiny heart divided into chambers. God became flesh.

Jesus entered our world not *like* a human but *as* a human. He endured puberty, pimples, hot weather, and cranky neighbors. God became human down to his very toes. He had suspended the stars and ladled out the seas, yet he suckled a breast and slept in hay.

Some years ago I wrote a chapter titled "Twenty-Five Questions for Mary," in which I imagined the ponderings that young Mary had about Jesus.[1] The idea captured the imagination of an elementary-school teacher. She asked her students to make a list of questions they would have liked to ask young Mary. Here are some of their responses:

"Could you believe that you were pregnant for the whole world?"

"Were you scared of not doing a good job?"

"What was Jesus' first word as a baby?"

"Was he beautiful?"

"Did he ever get sick?"

"Did Jesus ever misbehave?"

"Was Jesus born with hair?"

"What was his favorite food?"

"Did you feel any holier?"

"Did he ever have a pet?"

These are legitimate questions. The fact that we can ask them raises a greater one.

Why such a journey? Why did God go so far?

Why did God go so far? He wants you to know that he gets you. He understands how you feel and has faced what you face.

A chief reason is this: he wants you to know that he gets you. He understands how you feel and has faced what you face. Jesus is not "out of touch with our reality. He's been through weakness and testing, experienced it all—all but the sin. So let's walk right up to him and get what he is so ready to give. Take the mercy, accept the help" (Heb. 4:15–16 MSG).

Since you know he understands, you can boldly go to him. Because of Bethlehem's miracle, you can answer these fundamental questions: Does God care if I'm sad? Look at the tear-streaked face of Jesus as he stands near Lazarus's tomb. Does God notice when I'm afraid? Note the resolve in the eyes of Jesus as he marches through the storm to rescue his friends. Does God know if I am ignored or rejected?

Find the answer in the compassionate eyes of Christ as he stands to defend the adulterous woman.[2]

"[Jesus] radiates God's own glory and expresses the very character of God" (Heb. 1:3 NLT). Jesus himself stated, "Anyone who has seen me has seen the Father" (John 14:9).

"Anyone who has seen me weep has seen the Father weep."

"Anyone who has seen me laugh has seen the Father laugh."

"Anyone who has seen me determined has seen the Father determined."

Would you like to see God? Take a look at Jesus.

In 1926 George Harley founded a medical mission among the Mano tribe of Liberia. The locals were receptive to the doctor and helped him construct a clinic and a chapel. Eventually Harley treated more than ten thousand patients a year. During the first five years, however, not one person from the tribe visited his chapel.

Shortly after the doctor and his wife arrived, she gave birth to Robert, their first child. The boy grew up on the edge of the forest. "He was the apple of our eye," Harley later said. "How we loved our little boy! But one day when he was almost five years old, I looked out the window of the medical dispensary and saw Bobby. He was running across the field but he fell down. Then he got up and ran some more and fell again. But this time he didn't get up. So I ran out and picked up the feverish body of my own little boy.

I held him in my arms and said, 'Bobby, don't worry. Your daddy knows how to treat that tropical fever. He's going to help you get better.'"

Dr. Harley tried every treatment he knew. But nothing helped. The fever raged, and in short order the disease took the boy's life. The parents were distraught with grief. The missionary went into his workshop and built a coffin. Harley placed Robert inside and nailed the lid. He lifted the coffin on his shoulder and walked toward the clearing to find a place to dig a grave. One of the old men in the village saw him and asked about the box. When Harley explained that his son had died, the old man offered to help him carry the coffin. Dr. Harley told a friend what happened next:

> So the old man took one end of the coffin and I took the other. Eventually we came to the clearing in the forest. We dug a grave there and laid Bobby in it. But when we had covered up the grave, I just couldn't stand it any longer . . . I fell down on my knees in the dirt and began to sob uncontrollably. My beloved son was dead, and there I was in the middle of an African jungle 8,000 miles from home and relatives. I felt so all alone.
>
> But when I started crying, the old man cocked his head in stunned amazement. He squatted down beside me and looked at me so intently. For a long time, he sat there listening to me cry. Then suddenly, he leaped to his feet and went running back up the trail through

the jungle, screaming, again and again, at the top of his voice, "White man, white man—he cries like one of us."[3]

That evening as Harley and his wife grieved in their cottage, there was a knock at the door. Harley opened it. There stood the chief and almost every man, woman, and child in the village. They were back again the next Sunday and filled the chapel to overflowing. They wanted to hear about Jesus.

Everything changed when the villagers saw the tears of the missionary.

Everything changes when we see the face of God.

He took on your face in the hope that you would see his.

He came with tears too. He knows the burden of a broken heart. He knows the sorrow this life can bring. He could have come as a shining light or a voice in the clouds, but he came as a person. Does God understand you? Find the answer in Bethlehem.

Gaze where Mary gazed. Look into God's face and be assured. If the King was willing to enter the world of animals and shepherds and swaddling clothes, don't you think he's willing to enter yours?

He took on your face in the hope that you would see his.

3

Saved from Ourselves

I tried to blame my behavior on the holiday traffic. The Thanksgiving weekend had turned the streets near the shopping mall into controlled chaos.

I tried to blame my misdeeds on my state of mind. I was driving to my in-laws' house, having spent most of the day helping to plan a funeral for Denalyn's ever-weakening mother.

I tried to blame my poor reaction on the reckless U-turn made by the teenager. He nearly clipped my bumper.

The traffic arrow invited me to make a right turn into the busy avenue. As I did, the teenager made a sudden, unexpected hairpin turn around the median. We nearly shared paint. I honked at him. I'll confess: my honk wasn't a polite "Ahem, excuse me. I am over here." It was long and strong and demanded, "Do you know what you almost did?"

He drove a low-riding, wide-wheeled, two-toned, exhaust-puffing jalopy that dated back to the eighties. It needed a muffler. It also needed a more mature passenger. As the car accelerated, a long arm came out of the passenger-side window and gave me a backhanded, one-fingered wave.

Grrr. I sped up.

Thanks to a traffic light I was soon side by side with the perpetrator. He still had his window down. I lowered mine. He looked up at me. He wore a baseball cap shoved over a mop of black hair. The brim of the cap faced sideways. So did the smirk on his face.

"You need to watch that wave, son."

In an ideal world he would have apologized, and I would have wished him a merry Christmas, and I wouldn't be telling you this story.

But the world is not ideal. When I told him to "watch that wave," he smirked even more and demanded, "Make me!"

Make me? When was the last time I heard someone say, "Make me"? Middle school? High school locker room? There was that scuffle after the graduation party. *Make me?* That's what teens say. Of course, he was a teen. He didn't have a whisker on him. He was a skinny, floppy-haired, testosterone-laden adolescent who was feeling his oats riding shotgun in his buddy's muscle car.

As for me, I am a sixty-year-old pastor who writes Christian books and speaks at conferences and feels a call to make the world a better place. I should have raised my window. But I didn't. I looked down at him, literally and metaphorically, and said with my own version of a smirk, "Now, what did you say?"

"Make me," he repeated.

The saints in heaven were saying, "Drive away, Lucado."

Common sense was urging, "Drive away, Lucado."

The better angels of the universe were prompting, "Drive away, Lucado."

I didn't listen. The dare of the punk activated the punk inside me, the punk I hadn't seen in decades. I snarled. "Okay, where do you want to go?"

His eyes widened to the size of hamburger patties. He couldn't believe I'd said that. I couldn't believe I'd said that. You can't believe I said that. When he realized I was serious, he became the same.

"Let's settle this at the shopping mall."

"Are you kidding?" I told him. "There are too many people in a shopping mall. Follow me." Whaaat? All of a sudden I was the expert on where to go to duke it out?

The light turned and I accelerated. In my side-view mirror I could see that the two boys were engaged in a heated exchange.

"What do you think?"

"I dunno. What do you think?"

"He looks pretty cranky."

"Yeah, he might have a weapon or sump'n."

By the time I reached the next stoplight, they were nowhere to be seen. They must have turned into the parking lot.

Boy, was I relieved. I drove the rest of the way to my

in-laws' house, asking myself, *Did you really just dare a kid to fight? Are you crazy?*

I'd like to blame my behavior on my state of mind, the stress of the traffic, the driver who nearly hit my car, or the passenger who pushed my buttons. But I can blame my bizarre behavior on only one thing. The punk inside me. For a few minutes at a stoplight near a shopping mall, I forgot who I was.

And I forgot who the teenager was. In that heated moment he wasn't someone's son. He wasn't a creation of God. He wasn't a miracle. He wasn't fearfully and wonderfully made. He was a disrespectful jerk, and I let him bring out the disrespectful jerk in me.

The Bible has a name for this punkish tendency—sin. The sinful nature is the stubborn, self-centered attitude that says, "My way or the highway." The sinful nature is all about self: pleasing self, promoting self, preserving self. Sin is selfish.

I have a sin nature.

So do you. (Merry Christmas.) Under the right circumstances you will do the wrong thing. You won't want to. You'll try not to, but you will. Why? You have a sin nature.

You were born with it. We all were. Our parents didn't teach us to throw temper tantrums; we were born with the skill. No one showed us how to steal a cookie from our sibling; we just knew. We never attended a class on pouting or passing the blame, but we could do both before we were out of our diapers. The heart of the human problem is the problem of the human heart.

The heart of the human problem is the problem of the human heart.

Each one of us entered the world with a sin nature. God entered the world to take it away. Christmas commemorates the day and the way God saved us from ourselves. Look carefully at the words the angel spoke to Joseph.

> Joseph son of David, do not be afraid to take Mary home as your wife, because what is conceived in her is from the Holy Spirit. She will give birth to a son, and you are to give him the name Jesus, because he will save his people from their sins. (Matt. 1:20–21)

We may not see the connection between the name *Jesus* and the phrase "save his people from their sins," but Joseph would have. He was familiar with the Hebrew language. The English name *Jesus* traces its origin to the Hebrew word *Yeshua*. *Yeshua* is a shortening of *Yehoshuah*, which means "Yahweh saves."[1]

27

Who was Jesus? *God* saves.

What did Jesus come to do? God *saves*.

God saves. Jesus was not just godly, godlike, God hungry, God focused, or God worshipping. He was God. Not merely a servant of God, instrument of God, or friend of God, but Jesus was God.

God *saves*, not God empathizes, cares, listens, helps, assists, or applauds. God saves. Specifically "he will save his people from their sins" (v. 21). Jesus came to save us, not just from politics, enemies, challenges, or difficulties. He came to save us from our own sins.

Jesus came to save us, not just from
politics, enemies, challenges, or difficulties.
He came to save us from our own sins.

Here's why. God has high plans for you and me. He is recruiting for himself a people who will populate heaven. God will restore his planet and his children to their garden of Eden splendor. It will be perfect. Perfect in splendor. Perfect in righteousness. Perfect in harmony.

One word describes heaven: *perfect*.

One word describes us: *imperfect*.

God's kingdom is perfect, but his children are not, so what is he to do? Abandon us? Start over? He could. But he loves us too much to do that.

Will he tolerate us with our sin nature? Populate heaven with rebellious, self-centered citizens? If so, how would heaven be heaven?

He had a greater plan. "God was pleased for all of himself to live in Christ" (Col. 1:19 NCV).

All the love of God was in Jesus. All the strength of God was in Jesus. All the compassion and power and devotion of God were, for a time, in the earthly body of a carpenter.

No wonder the winds obeyed when Jesus spoke; he was *God speaking*.

No wonder the bacteria fled when Jesus touched the wounds; he was *God touching*.

No wonder the water held him as he walked; he was *God walking*.

No wonder the people stood speechless as he taught; he was *God teaching*.

And no wonder ten thousand angels stood in rapt attention as Jesus was nailed to the cross; he was *God dying*.

He let people crucify him, for goodness' sake! He became sin for our sake. "He made Him who knew no sin to be sin for us" (2 Cor. 5:21 NKJV). What started in the Bethlehem cradle culminated on the Jerusalem cross.

But that's not all.

Jesus not only did a work *for* us; he does a work *within*

us. "The mystery in a nutshell is just this: Christ is in you" (Col. 1:27 MSG).

He commandeers our hands and feet, requisitions our minds and tongues. "He decided from the outset to shape the lives of those who love him along the same lines as the life of his Son" (Rom. 8:29 MSG).

Having paid sin's penalty, Christ defuses sin's power. The punk within diminishes, and the Christ within flourishes. God changes us day by day from one level to the next. We'll never be sinless, but we will sin less.

We'll never be sinless, but we will sin less.

And when we do sin, we have this assurance: the grace that saved us also preserves us. We may lose our tempers, our perspective, and our self-control. But we never lose our hope. Why? Because God has his hold on us. He "is able to keep you from stumbling, and to present you faultless before the presence of His glory with exceeding joy" (Jude v. 24 NKJV).

The believer has been saved from the guilt of sin, is being saved from problems of sin, and, upon the return of Christ, will be saved from the punishment for sin. Complete and full-service salvation.

God saves!

And *only* God saves. If we could save ourselves, why would we need a Savior? Jesus did not enter the world to help us save ourselves. He entered the world to save us from ourselves.

As a Boy Scout, I earned a lifesaving merit badge. I never actually saved anyone. In fact, the only people I saved were other Boy Scouts who didn't need to be saved. During training I would rescue other trainees. We took turns saving each other. But since we weren't really drowning, we resisted being rescued.

"Stop kicking and let me save you," I'd say.

It's impossible to save those who are trying to save themselves.

You might save yourself from a broken heart or going broke or running out of gas. But you aren't good enough to save yourself from sin. You aren't strong enough to save yourself from death. You need a Savior.

Because of Bethlehem you have one.

You need a Savior. Because of Bethlehem you have one.

When you say yes to him, he says yes to you. He will change your sin nature into his nature. Good to know, especially in holiday traffic.

If perchance these words find their way to a couple of brash kids who recognize this story, to you I say, "I'm sorry. Your actions were wrong, but my reaction was worse. God is working on us all."

4

Hope for the Hole-idays

Christmas is a season of interruptions. Some we enjoy. Some we don't.

We enjoy interrupting diets for eggnog, work for a staff party, and bill paying for Christmas cards.

But we could do without the Chicago snowstorm that grounds the Atlanta flight, which strands the passengers in Albuquerque. We could do without the midnight phone call from Cousin Bert saying that he and Mary Lou and their kids are going to be in the area for the holidays. Could they park their Winnebago in the driveway for "Oh, we promise, no more than ten days"?

Interruptions. They come with Christmas. They come with life.

Just when you sell the crib—surprise! Another child. Just when you're ready to retire—surprise! More tuition. Just when you thought your plans were finalized—surprise! More layoffs, surgery, transfers, or treatments.

Interruptions. They can stir fear and anxiety. They steal

our sleep and pickpocket our joy. They can cause us to question God, even turn away from God.

You may be facing an interruption in this season of life. What you wanted and what you received do not match. And now you are troubled and anxious, even angry. Does that describe you?

It certainly described our family last Christmas.

It was the second weekend of the Advent season. I'd spent the day preparing for and speaking at a Saturday night church service. By the time I arrived home, it was well into the evening hours. Denalyn was waiting for me in the kitchen. I could tell by her expression that something was wrong.

"Max, Jenna is pregnant."

Her announcement did not match her demeanor. Denalyn should have been waving her arms and hugging me. Grandparents at last! But there was no confetti, just concern. Her eyes were tear filled.

"She's in the emergency room."

We raced to the hospital.

Emergency rooms do not wear Christmas decorations well. A garland does not make an X-ray machine festive. Red and green bulbs cannot shed a happy glow on a gurney. No matter the song on the intercom, the monitors beep louder than the sleigh bells ring. An ER is still an ER. Even at Christmas. And our daughter was in the ER.

A nurse led us down the hallway into a room. Jenna

was on the bed. She tried to be stoic and succeeded, for about ten seconds. Then she began to cry. She had wanted to surprise the family. She wanted to make a big deal out of a Christmas pregnancy. She wanted to have a baby.

By the end of the night, we knew that wasn't likely.

By the next morning the doctor assured us it wasn't to be.

It had already been a tough season for Jenna and her husband, Brett. His dad had died a month earlier. Their November was gray with sorrow. Now December was going to be even more so.

Jenna said her Christmas felt more like a hole-iday than a holiday.

Maybe yours feels the same. More tear than cheer. More yuck than yule.

- The sight of happy children is a reminder of a vacant crib.
- The busy social schedule of some only highlights your empty one.
- Images of families together reinforce your pain of a family apart.

If this season is hard for you, if you're looking forward to December 26 more than December 25, then I have a story for you to consider. A story of a young girl.

As much as she tried to keep a good attitude, it was not

easy. She was far from home, miles from family and her own bed. She had spent the last few days on crowded roads, enduring the winter chill. Money was scarce. Friends were nowhere near. A warm bed and a hot meal? The prospects were slim.

Ask her which was worse, the pain in her heart or the pain in her back, and she'd be hard pressed to make a choice.

Her heart ached for her family. She felt estranged from them. Under normal circumstances they would have been thrilled to learn of her pregnancy. But pregnant before the wedding? With her conservative family and her bizarre explanation? And to have to tell the man she was to marry that she was carrying a child who wasn't his? It was a miracle he still married her. And another miracle was what she needed that night.

She'd envisioned giving birth at home: Mom holding one hand, an aunt the other; a midwife, doting relatives, Joseph, and a crowd of neighbors outside the door. Perhaps if they all could have experienced the birth of her firstborn together, then they would believe her story.

At least that's how I imagine Mary felt. Of course, I could be wrong. Perhaps the feed trough and stable were her idea. But I don't think so. I've yet to meet a mother-to-be who dreams of using a cow stall for a delivery room and a manger for a bassinet. I doubt Mary did either. So when Joseph returned from the inn and asked if she was allergic to sheep, it's a safe hunch to say she was chagrined. This wasn't how she had planned to celebrate the birth of Jesus.

Joseph led the donkey down a steep path that ended at the mouth of a cave carved out years before by the wind and the rain, used as long as anyone could remember for a barn. He lowered Mary off the back of the donkey. He looked at her face, fatigued and powdery from the road. He apologized for the austere accommodations. She touched his cheek and smiled and entered the grotto.

Joseph built a fire and heated water. Mary cleared a spot on the straw and set about the task of bringing God into the world. With cows as her witnesses and Joseph as her midwife, she did just that.

Within moments the hand of the Star Hanger clutched Mary's finger. The feet of the Sky Walker lay in Joseph's palm. No wonder the angels filled the sky with worship. Any doubt of the Father's love disappeared the night God was wrapped in barnyard towels so the hay wouldn't scratch his back.

Any doubt of the Father's love disappeared the night God was wrapped in barnyard towels so the hay wouldn't scratch his back.

In that moment Mary knew it was all worth it. The ache in her back, the ache in her heart—they faded away. The questions of how, the wonderings of when—they didn't linger. The inn had no place for her son; that was all right. He would find a place in people's hearts. She and Joseph were far from home on the night of Jesus' birth; that was all right. Jesus was even farther from his. There was no warm bed in which Jesus could sleep? No problem.

In spite of the chaos, Christ came.

Through a scandalous pregnancy, an imposed census, an untimely trip, and an overcrowded inn, God triumphed in Mary's story.

And he triumphed in Matthew's genealogy. We don't often mention the lineage of Jesus in context with his birth. Matthew did, however. He opens his gospel with a list with dozens of names. Before he presents the wise men and the star of Bethlehem, he tells us that "Abraham begot Isaac, Isaac begot Jacob, and Jacob begot Judah and his brothers. Judah begot Perez and Zerah by Tamar, Perez begot Hezron, and Hezron begot Ram" (Matt. 1:2–3 NKJV).

The list goes on and on (and on) for sixteen verses. "Obed begot Jesse, and Jesse begot David the king. David the king begot Solomon" (vv. 5–6 NKJV). *Yawn*. Let's skip to the nativity story! Who needs to know about Tamar, Rahab, and Ruth? Why does Matthew mention David and Solomon before he mentions Joseph and Mary?

He is making a point. Chaos cannot keep Christ out of his world. The Messiah was born not because of his ancestors but in spite of them. Tamar was abandoned. Ruth was an immigrant, and Rahab was a harlot. David was an adulterer. Solomon was a philanderer. The family tree of Jesus is gnarled and crooked. Some of the kings were bloodthirsty and godless. Yet God had promised that Jesus would come, and Jesus came. Hence the triumphant conclusion of the genealogy:

> Jacob was the father of Joseph, who married a woman named Mary. It was Mary who gave birth to Jesus, and it is Jesus who is the Savior, the Anointed One. (v. 16 *The Voice*)

Christ came!
In spite of sin and scandal, Christ came.
In spite of racism and sexism, Christ came.
Though the people forgot God, Christ came.
In spite of, and out of, the pandemonium, Christ came.
The surprise pregnancy, the sudden census, the long road from Nazareth to Bethlehem. Unpleasant and difficult, yet they resulted in the world's greatest miracle. "And [Mary] brought forth her firstborn Son, and wrapped Him in swaddling cloths, and laid Him in a manger" (Luke 2:7 NKJV). Everything before this happened so this moment would happen. Was the first Christmas different from what Mary had planned? Yes, but it turned out greater than she could have dreamed. God used the struggles to accomplish his will.

Don't you need that reminder? In your world of short

nights, hard work, and high stress, don't you need to know that Jesus holds it all together?

You might relate to the jalopy I once saw. The car clattered down the freeway, one door missing, hood dented, needing paint. On the loosely hanging bumper was this sticker: "Honk if anything falls off."

"For everything, absolutely everything, above and below, visible and invisible, rank after rank after rank of angels—*everything* got started in him and finds its purpose in him. He was there before any of it came into existence and holds it all together right up to this moment" (Col. 1:16–17 MSG).

You cannot face a crisis if you don't face God first.

God holds it all together. And he will hold it together for you.

Everything inside you and every voice around you says, "Get out. Get angry. Get drunk. Get high." But don't listen to the voices. You cannot face a crisis if you don't face God first.

Don't worry about anything; instead, pray about everything; tell God your needs, and don't forget to thank him for his answers. If you do this, you will experience God's peace, which is far more wonderful than the human mind can understand. His peace will keep your thoughts and your hearts quiet and at rest as you trust in Christ Jesus. (Phil. 4:6–7 TLB)

Cling to him. In the ER, when your dreams are falling apart, say to him, "Lord, I need you now." Between the headstones of the cemetery, whisper, "Dear Jesus, lift me up." During the deposition, when others are grumbling beneath their breath, may you be overheard repeating this prayer: "God, you are good. I . . . need . . . help. Encourage me, please."

In the prayer journal of King David, we read this question: "When all that is good falls apart, what can good people do?" (Ps. 11:3 NCV).

Isn't David's question ours? When all that is good falls apart, what can good people do?

When terrorists attack, when diseases rage, when families collapse, when churches divide . . . when all that is good falls apart, what can good people do? What is the godly response to the unexpected mishaps and calamities of life?

Curiously, David didn't answer his question with an answer. He answered it with a declaration. "The LORD is in his holy temple. The LORD is on his throne in heaven" (v. 4 NIrV).

His point is unmistakable: When everything shakes,

God remains unshaken. He is in his holy temple. His plan will not be derailed. God is unaffected by our storms. He is undeterred by our problems.

When everything shakes, God remains unshaken.

Remember the story of Jacob's son Joseph in Egypt? Look at him in the prison. His brothers sold him out; Potiphar's wife turned him in. If ever a world caved in, Joseph's did.

Or consider Moses, watching flocks in the wilderness. Was this what he intended to do with his life? Hardly. His heart beat with Jewish blood. His passion was to lead the slaves, so why did God have him leading sheep?

And Daniel? He was among the brightest and best young men of Israel—the equivalent of a West Point Cadet or Ivy Leaguer. But he and his entire generation were being marched out of Jerusalem into Babylonian captivity. The city was destroyed. The temple was in ruins.

Joseph in prison. Moses in the desert. Daniel in chains. These were dark moments. Who could have seen any good in them? Who could have known that Joseph the prisoner was just one promotion from becoming Joseph the prime minister? Who would have thought that God was giving Moses forty years of wilderness training in the very desert through which he would lead the people? And who could have imagined that Daniel, the captive, would soon be Daniel the king's counselor?

God has made a business out of turning tragedy into triumph. He did with Joseph, with Moses, with Daniel, and, most of all, he did with Jesus on the cross. The innocent one was slaughtered. Heaven's gift was murdered. Mothers wept, evil danced, and the apostles had to wonder, "When all that is good falls apart, what do good people do?"

God answered their question with a declaration, with the rumble of the earth and the rolling of the rock. He reminded them, "The LORD is in his holy temple. The LORD is on his throne in heaven" (Ps. 11:4 NIrv).

Is your Christmas a difficult one? Then take heart. God is still in his temple, still on his throne, still in control. And he still makes princes out of prisoners, counselors out of captives, Sundays out of Fridays, and he still brings beauty out of Bethlehems.

He did then, for them. He does it still, for you and me.

5

It's Never Too Late

The gift is hidden in my sock drawer. It's nestled in the back right corner between the blacks and the browns. Denalyn will open the box on Christmas morning. The room will fill with the sound of oohs and aahs. She will clasp the chain around her neck and display the pendant and smile at her husband. One of our daughters will exclaim, "What a perfect gift!" Another will ask, "Dad, how did you know?"

It was easy. I took the hint. When Denalyn made her Christmas wishes known, I took her wishes home and hid them in my sock drawer. I'll get great reviews. But the truth? Denalyn all but bought her gift.

She escorted me into the mall jewelry store and asked the salesclerk to pull the pendant out of the glass counter. She held the chain against her neck and examined the medallion in the mirror on the counter. She then spoke to me, pacing her speech as one might with a non-English speaker. "Max . . . I . . . like . . . this . . ."

The woman behind the counter joined in. "I think your

wife likes this necklace, product number 251, in case you ever need to know."

"Max, are you listening?"

I wasn't. I was gazing out at the foot traffic, noting the large number of people wearing football jerseys, which reminded me of Sunday's big game, a must-win for the Dallas Cowboys if they were going to make the play-offs. That thought prompted a mental review of my calendar. *Will I be home for the game? Do we have snacks? I love to eat barbecue potato chips during a game. In fact, I'd love some right now. Does anyone in this mall sell them?*

"Max." The voice came from a distant place.

"Max." It sounded familiar.

"Max!" That's when I remembered where I was. (I never got the chips.)

I turned. Denalyn was looking at me. The salesclerk was looking at me. I had a feeling that every female in sight was looking at me. Hints began dropping like snow in a Winnipeg winter.

Denalyn to me: "Christmas is next month, Max."

Salesclerk: "You can pick this up at any point, Mr. Lucado."

Denalyn to salesclerk: "What was the product number again?"

Salesclerk to Denalyn: "Number 251."

Denalyn to me: "Let me write that down just in

case someone I married needs help with his
shopping list."

Salesclerk to me: "We are open until 9:00 p.m."

Denalyn to me: "They are open until 9:00 p.m."

I just nodded and smiled. Truth be told, I need all the
nudges I can get. If only every decision in life were this easy.
All I did was pay attention.

Oh, that the same could be said about the innkeeper.
He could have witnessed the birth of Jesus. All he needed
to do was make room for the couple from Nazareth. But he
didn't. And because he didn't, Scripture contains these sad
lines:

> While they were in Bethlehem, the time came for
> Mary to have the baby, and she gave birth to her
> first son. Because there were no rooms left in the
> inn, she wrapped the baby with pieces of cloth and
> laid him in a feeding trough. (Luke 2:6–7 NCV)

So much is left unsaid in this passage. We know nothing
about the innkeeper or the inn or the time of day. What we
do know is this: he did not invite them in. There was no
vacancy. The census turned sleepy Bethlehem into a boom-
town. The innkeeper filled every room and closet. He placed
someone in every bed, an occupant in every cot. He lined the
hallways with mats and rollaways. The place was crowded.

But, honestly, couldn't he have found one more space? Mary was third-trimester pregnant. Wouldn't you find a bed for a mother-to-be? Of course you would. Which makes me wonder, was there another reason Jesus' parents were turned away?

Maybe the knock on the door was at midnight. The last candle had been snuffed out, the last dish washed. The only sound was the popping of the fireplace coals and the snoring of the slumbering guests. The innkeeper answered the door wearing his nightshirt. Through a six-inch opening he peered into the dark and told Joseph, "It's too late. We're all bedded down. Earlier there might have been room. Earlier I might have made room. But at this hour? I'm sorry."

Besides, Mary's pregnancy might prove problematic. What if she screamed during labor and woke up the other guests? And the baby? Babies can be noisy, restless. This was a hotel, not a maternity ward.

Perhaps the hour was too late.

Or the couple was too common.

Simple villagers, they were. Hoi polloi. Had Mary and Joseph been Queen Mary and King Joseph, the innkeeper would have responded differently. Had they arrived with camels and servants instead of a few clothes and a tired donkey—had they been uncommon—the response of the innkeeper might have been uncommon. But no trumpet sounded. No herald proclaimed. No courier announced their arrival. There was only a knock.

A knock at the door . . .
   by a common couple . . .
      at a late hour . . .
         when the inn was crowded.
So the innkeeper missed the opportunity.

The innkeeper missed the opportunity. Many still do.

Many still do. They miss the chance to open the door. They let the birth of Jesus pass them by. The miracle of Bethlehem still happens. God enters the hamlets of our lives and speaks to us. He speaks through scriptures, sunsets, the kindness of a friend, or the warning of a medical report. He sings to us through Christmas carols. He calls to us through Christmas sermons. He reaches out through the Christmas story.

"Here I am!" Jesus invites. "I stand at the door and knock. If you hear my voice and open the door, I will come in and eat with you, and you will eat with me" (Rev. 3:20 NCV).

I have a friend who works with churches in Papua New Guinea. Many in their culture don't knock on doors. They stand at the doorframe and politely cough to announce their presence. When Bible translators tried to explain the idea of Jesus knocking on the door, it made no sense to the locals.

The missionaries solved the cross-cultural problem by rendering the verse "I stand at the door and cough."

Whether Jesus is clearing his throat or tapping on the door, the point is the same. He is gentle and polite. He never forces his way in. Yet just as we reach to open the door, the baby cries, the phone rings, the timer goes off, or the beep on the automated calendar reminds us to study for the exam, call the doctor, do the laundry, or cut the grass.

Life is crowded. Your life is crowded. Heaven knows, you already have more than you can do. And because heaven knows, Jesus comes not with a list of things for you to do but with a list of things he has already done and will do. Your death? Defeated. Your sins? Forgiven. Your fears? He will give you courage. Your questions? He will guide you.

Jesus lifts burdens; he doesn't add to them.

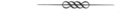

Jesus comes not with a list of things for you to do but with a list of things he has already done and will do. Jesus lifts burdens; he doesn't add to them.

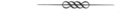

"But it's too late," you say. No it isn't. It's never too late for Christ.

You are never too old, too messed up, or too worn-out. Elijah was depressed. God still came to him. Abraham was old. God still led him. Moses was long retired. God still called him. Jonah was on the run. God still used him. Jacob cheated his family. God still had a place for him. Peter betrayed Christ, Saul persecuted Christ, Thomas doubted Christ, but each learned it was not too late for Christ.

It's never too late to come to Christ for help.

I was called to the bedside of a dying man a few days back, an eighty-year-old scoundrel. Yes, a scoundrel! He spent the final decade of his life with time on his hands, money at his disposal, and women on his mind. His exploits would have made Hugh Hefner blush. But as his health began to fail, his conscience began to stir. When the doctor told him to get his affairs in order, he called me. He wanted to get right with God. He made a deathbed confession of faith.

Might I make a confession of my own? I left the hospital room with a scroogy scowl. *That's too easy,* I thought. *A guy like him deserves to be routed through purgatory on the way to paradise.*

But God didn't tell me to screen the applicants, just to teach them. And according to God's great grace, if my scoundrel friend's confession was sincere, he is walking the same heavenly streets as Paul and Peter and King David. Each a scoundrel in his own right.

It's never too late to come to Christ for help. Your stack of sins is never too high. Your list of failures is never too long. That knock at the door of your heart? That's Jesus.

It's one thing to miss a message from your spouse, but to miss a message from God? That's a mistake you don't want to make.

All you have to do is open the door.

6

Worship Works Wonders

Dear Ladies,

We know you mean well. We know you think you know best. But enough is enough. We have suffered in silence for too long. Having shared our pain with one another, we husbands hereby step out of the shadows and open our hearts. This year as you shop for our Christmas gifts, please don't buy us what we need.

We know we need to smell better and look nicer. We know you like us in warm pajamas and new underwear. But we do not know what to say when we open these gifts. How can you fake enthusiasm over house slippers? How can you look happy holding a nose-hair trimmer? We've lied long enough. For the sake of integrity on Christmas morning, we offer this guidance. As you look at any potential gift, ask yourself these questions: Can he play with it? Does it swing, bounce, shuffle, cast, or roll? Can you find a trigger, grip, rip cord, or stick shift? Does it consume oil or dog food? Does it have a big screen and a remote control? If it does, buy it. Doesn't matter that he already has one. This is no time to be practical.

When considering an item of men's apparel, ask yourself, is it brown and green and rain resistant? You can't lose with any garment that is. Realizing that many women prefer to shop anywhere but the gun department, we offer these two questions. Does it make him look cute? Does it make him look like a hunk? If the clothing makes him look cute, drop it immediately. If it makes him look like a hunk, buy two.

When all else fails, ask, can he eat it? Note, the question is not, would you eat it? Or do other humans eat it? Or is it edible? Don't occupy yourself with trivialities. The question is, can he eat it? Anytime the answer is affirmative, consider yourself on safe ground.

In closing we extend this offer. If you will buy us what we want, we will do the same for you. Without revealing any details we will tell you this. A large vacuum cleaner company has offered us a group discount. (And you thought we were insensitive.)

No need to thank us,
Your husbands

hristmas and gift giving. The two have always been associated with each other for good reason. The magi gave Jesus the gifts of gold, frankincense, and myrrh. The shepherds gave Jesus the gift of their time and belief. Mary gave Jesus the gift of her womb. The offerings seem practical. The wise men's treasures could be used to fund the family's escape to Egypt. The shepherds' visitation would keep the family company. Mary's womb would protect the growing child. But there is one gift that might appear a bit curious.

The angels' gift of worship.

> Suddenly, the angel was joined by a vast host of others—the armies of heaven—praising God:
>
> "Glory to God in the highest heaven," they sang, "and peace on earth for all those pleasing him."
>
> When this great army of angels had returned again to heaven, the shepherds said to each other, "Come on! Let's go to Bethlehem! Let's see this wonderful thing that has happened, which the Lord has told us about." (Luke 2:13–15 TLB)

The angels filled the night with light and the air with music, and, well, that's it. They worshipped. Couldn't they have done something more useful? Mary could have used a bed. Joseph would have benefited from an angelic escort back to Nazareth. Baby Jesus needed a bassinet.

These were angels. Didn't they know better?

Then again, these were angels. Who knew Jesus better than they? Those who knew Jesus best loved him dearest. Those who had followed him the longest gave him the gift of worship. They placed their love on a pillow of praise and presented it to Jesus. They did that night. They do so still. Heaven at this very moment reverberates with loud corporate worship. "Day and night they never stop saying: 'Holy, holy, holy'" (Rev. 4:8).

The word *worship* actually evolved from the Old English word *weorthscipe*. "To worship, then, is to ascribe worth to someone or something."[1]

Worship happens anytime you turn your heart toward heaven and say, "You are worthy." When you clear your calendar for prayer, turn the radio dial to praise music, or use your morning jog to recite Bible verses or your lunch break to meditate, this is worship.

Worship happens in neighborhoods, in living rooms, in open pastures. And, yes, worship happens in churches. When the people of God make a public and plural declaration of God's goodness, worship is happening.

God is on the hunt for those who will imitate the angels, for people who will open their hearts and mouths and declare, "Glory to God in the highest heaven." "The Father . . . is actively seeking such people to worship him" (John 4:23 NCV).

Perhaps you are wondering, *But what if I don't worship?*

Oh, but you will. The question is not, will you worship? The question is, where will you direct your worship? We all worship someone or something. Why, I once worshipped a bicycle!

At the age of eight I asked my parents to give me a bicycle for Christmas. Not just any bike but a fire-engine red Schwinn bike with a banana seat and high handlebars. They did! Basking in the light of the Christmas tree, it beckoned me to climb aboard and ride away into the bliss of childhood.

I decorated the handlebars with tassels and bought a reflector for the fender. I attached a playing card to the frame so it would *click, click, click* against the tire spokes. I was cool. James Dean–level cool. My bike and I explored subdivisions, drainage ditches, and dirt roads. I loved the bike. I *worshipped* the bike.

But then I wrecked it. I crashed into a curb and bent the frame. My dad and I tried to repair it, but the bike was never the same. It let me down. I was counting on it to carry me, to deliver me, to entertain me, to fulfill me. It didn't.

What about you? You were counting on that career to carry you, deliver you, entertain you, and fulfill you. But it hasn't.

You were counting on that marriage to carry you, deliver you, entertain you, and fulfill you. But it didn't.

You were counting on that retirement to carry you, deliver you, entertain you, and fulfill you. But it hasn't.

You were counting on that education to carry you, deliver you, entertain you, and fulfill you. But it didn't.

You were counting on that body to carry you, deliver you, entertain you, and fulfill you. But it hasn't.

Worship might not be the word you've used to describe your passion, yet the term fits. Anytime we trust an object or activity to give us life and meaning, we worship it.

> When we make good things the
> ultimate things, we set ourselves
> up for disappointment.

When we make good things the ultimate things, we set ourselves up for disappointment. If we depend on a career or relationship to give our lives meaning, what happens when retirement comes or the relationship ends? The list of impostor gods includes sex, food, money, alcohol, success, and influence. In the correct dosage and context, these can be wonderful gifts from God. But they are dismal substitutes for God. To worship them is to be satisfied, then brokenhearted. Infatuated, then discouraged. Enthralled, then angry.

God-centered worship rescues us from bamboozlers, trompe l'oeil gods who never deliver on their promises. Worship does to the soul what a spring rain does to a thirsty field. It soaks down, seeps in, and stirs life. Are you stressed? Worship God, who could store the universe in his pocket and the oceans in an eyedropper. Are you ashamed? Worship Jesus, whose love never fades. Are you bereaved? Open your heart to your Shepherd. He will lead you through the valley of sorrow. Do you feel small? A few moments in front of the throne of your loving King will evaporate any sense of insignificance. Worship works wonders.

For your own sake do what the angels did: make a big deal about the arrival of the King.

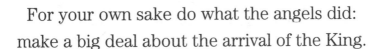

For your own sake do what the angels did: make a big deal about the arrival of the King.

Worship verbally. "Through Jesus, therefore, let us continually offer to God a sacrifice of praise—the fruit of lips that openly profess his name" (Heb. 13:15).

In the early eighties there was a popular country song entitled "Always on My Mind."[2] The singer tells his sweetheart that even though he seldom expressed his feelings through words or actions, she was always on his mind. I'm not sure where the writer of those lyrics learned the secret of romance, but he didn't consult women. No sweetheart would accept that excuse. "You never told me, never gave me flowers, kind words, or compliments, but I was always on your mind? Yeah, right."

God doesn't buy it either. He wants to hear our affection. It is out of the abundance of the heart that the mouth speaks,[3] and when the mouth is silent, the heart is in question. Do you love God? Let him know. Tell him! Out loud. In public. Unashamed. Let there be jubilation, celebration, and festivity! "Shout to God with joyful praise!" (Ps. 47:1 NLT). "Make a joyful shout to God, all the earth!" (Ps. 66:1 NKJV).

John Wesley wrote, "Sing lustily, and with a good courage. Beware of singing as if you were half dead, or half asleep; but lift up your voice with strength. Be no more afraid of your voice now, nor more ashamed of its being heard, than when you sung the songs of Satan."[4]

Speaking of Satan, he cannot tolerate Christ-centered worship. Unlike God, he is not omniscient. Satan cannot read your mind. He is not moved by what you think, only by what you say. So say it! "Yell a loud *no* to the Devil and watch him scamper. Say a quiet *yes* to God and he'll be there in no time" (James 4:7–8 MSG). Do you want your city to be free from Satan's grip? Worship! Do you want your home to be loosed from the Devil? Worship! Do we want nations to be places of peace and prosperity? Then let the church assault Satan's strongholds with joy-filled praise. Worship verbally. And . . .

Worship in community. "There was . . . a *multitude* of the heavenly host praising God" (Luke 2:13 NKJV, emphasis mine). The presence of Christ deserves an abundant chorus. Every generation has its share of "Jesus, yes; church, no"

Christians. For a variety of reasons they turn away from church attendance. They do so at a great loss. Something happens in corporate worship that does not happen in private worship. When you see my face in the sanctuary and I hear your voice in the chorus, we are mutually edified. Granted, congregational worship is imperfect. We often sing off-key. Our attention tends to wander. The preacher stumbles over his words, and the organist misses her cue. Even so, let us worship. The sincerity of our worship matters more than the quality. "Let's see how inventive we can be in encouraging love and helping out, not avoiding worshiping together as some do but spurring each other on, especially as we see the big Day approaching" (Heb. 10:24–25 MSG).

Worship demonstrably. Let your body express what your heart is feeling. And let your heart be awakened by your body. "May the lifting up of my hands be like the evening sacrifice" (Ps. 141:2). "Because your love is better than life, my lips will glorify you. I will praise you as long as I live, and in your name I will lift up my hands" (Ps. 63:3–4).

Yes, outward expressions of worship can be used inappropriately. People show off. They strut. They worship to be seen. But don't let potential abuse preclude appropriate use. Lift your hands. Clap your hands. Bend your knees. Bow your head. Fall down on your face.

Something powerful happens when we worship.

Something powerful happened the day that the soldiers did. It was Christmas Eve 1915 near the village of Laventie in northern France. World War I was raging. Bombs shook the soil of Europe. Frigid temperatures shook the bones of the fighters. Germans were entrenched on one side and the Royal Welsh Fusiliers on the other. Most of the soldiers were only a few years removed from boyhood. They were young, homesick, and longing to be with loved ones. The guns had blazed in relentless fury for months. Christmas seemed far away from this blood-soaked land.

At one point from the German side of the field came a chorus of voices singing a Welsh holiday hymn in German.

> Sleep my child and peace attend thee,
> All through the night
> Guardian angels God will send thee,
> All through the night
> Soft the drowsy hours are creeping
> Hill and vale in slumber sleeping,
> I my loving vigil keeping
> All through the night.[5]

Soldiers on both sides set down their weapons. For a moment, in that moment, there was no war; there were no enemies; there was just the song. What happened next could only be described as a miracle. The night was spent in carol singing. Around dawn the feelings of goodwill emboldened the soldiers to step out of their trenches and greet their foes. Shouting such greetings as "Hello, Tommy" and "Hello,

Fritz," they shook hands in no-man's-land and exchanged gifts. German beer, sausages, and spiked helmets from one side. Canned corned beef, biscuits, and tunic buttons from the other.

Then, of all things, a game broke out. A form of soccer. It was disjointed and unorganized with perhaps as many as fifty players on each side. For half an hour or so, the battlefield became a soccer field, and enemies enjoyed time together.[6]

And it all began with worship.

We can only pray that an armistice would happen again. That warriors would become worshippers. That we would lay down our weapons of pride and vengeance and join hearts to thank the One who came to bring peace on earth and goodwill to all.

Someday that peace will come. Conflict will give way to an eternal chorus. Until then, we can practice.

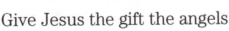

Give Jesus the gift the angels
gave him, the gift of praise.

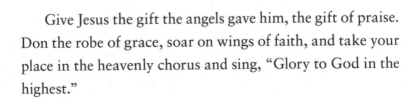

Give Jesus the gift the angels gave him, the gift of praise. Don the robe of grace, soar on wings of faith, and take your place in the heavenly chorus and sing, "Glory to God in the highest."

7

God Guides the Wise

oliday time is highway time. Ever since the magi packed their bags for Bethlehem, the birth of Jesus has caused people to hit the road. Our Christmas trips have a lot in common with the one of the wise men. We don't camp with camels, but we have been known to bump into a knobby-kneed in-law on the way to the bathroom. We don't keep an eye out for star lights, but flashing lights of the highway patrol? We watch for them at every curve. And we don't ride in a spice-road caravan, but six hours in a minivan with four kids might have made the wise men thankful for animals.

It's not always ho ho ho on the high, high highway. Extended time in the car reveals human frailties.

Dads refuse to stop. They hearken back to the examples of their forefathers. Did the pioneers spend the night at a Holiday Inn? Did Lewis and Clark ask for directions? Did Joseph allow Mary to stroll through a souvenir shop on the road to Bethlehem? By no means. Men drive as if they have a biblical mandate to travel far and fast, stopping only for gasoline.

And children? Road trips do to kids what a full moon does to the wolf man. If one child says, "I like that song," you might expect the other to say, "That's nice." Won't happen. Instead the other child will reply, "It stinks and so do your feet."

There is also the issue of JBA—juvenile bladder activity. A child can go weeks without going to the bathroom at home. But once on the road, the kid starts leaking like secrets in Washington. On one drive to Colorado, my daughters visited every toilet in New Mexico.

The best advice for traveling with young children is to be thankful they aren't teenagers. Teens are embarrassed by what their parents say, think, wear, eat, and sing. So for their sakes (and if you ever want to see your future grandchildren), don't smile at the waitstaff, don't breathe, and don't sing with the window down or up.

It's wiser to postpone traveling with children until they are a more reasonable age—like forty-two.

Christmas and travel. The first has a way of prompting the second and has done so ever since the delegation from the distant land came searching for Jesus.

Jesus was born in Bethlehem in Judea, during the reign of King Herod. About that time some wise men from eastern lands arrived in Jerusalem, asking,

"Where is the newborn king of the Jews?" (Matt. 2:1–2 NLT)

Matthew loved the magi. He gave their story more square inches of text than he gave the narrative of the birth of Jesus. He never mentions the shepherds or the manger, but he didn't want us to miss the star and the seekers. It's easy to see why. Their story is our story. We're all travelers, all sojourners. In order to find Jesus, every one of us needs direction. God gives it. The story of the wise men shows us how.

> In order to find Jesus, every one of us needs direction. God gives it.

We have seen His star in the East and have come to worship Him. (v. 2 NKJV)

God uses the natural world to get our attention. Earth and stars form the first missionary society. "The heavens declare the glory of God" (Ps. 19:1 NKJV). As Paul wrote, "The basic reality of God is plain enough. Open your eyes and there it is! By taking a long and thoughtful look at what God has created, people have always been able to see what their eyes as such can't see: eternal power, for instance, and the mystery of his divine being" (Rom. 1:19–20 MSG).

God led the wise men to Jerusalem with a star. But to lead them to Jesus, he used something else:

King Herod was deeply disturbed when he heard this, as was everyone in Jerusalem. He called a meeting of the leading priests and teachers of religious law and asked, "Where is the Messiah supposed to be born?"

"In Bethlehem in Judea," they said, "for this is what the prophet wrote:

'And you, O Bethlehem in the land of Judah,
    are not least among the ruling cities of Judah,
for a ruler will come from you
    who will be the shepherd for my people Israel.'"
(Matt. 2:3–6 NLT)

The star sign was enough to lead the magi to Jerusalem. But it took Scripture to lead them to Jesus.

People see signs of God every day. Sunsets that steal the breath. Newborns that bring tears. Migrating geese that stir a smile. But do all who see the signs draw near to God? No. Many are content simply to see the signs. They do not realize that the riches of God are intended to turn us toward him. "Perhaps you do not understand that God is kind to you so you will change your hearts and lives" (Rom. 2:4 NCV).

The wise men, however, understood the purpose of the sign.

They followed it to Jerusalem, where they heard about the scripture. The prophecy told them where to find Christ. It is interesting to note that the star reappeared *after* they learned about the prophecy. The star "came and stood shining *right over* the place where the Child was" (Matt. 2:9, emphasis mine).[1] It is as if the sign and word worked together to bring the wise men to Jesus. The ultimate aim of all God's messages, both miraculous and written, is to shed the light of heaven on Jesus.

The ultimate aim of all God's messages, both miraculous and written, is to shed the light of heaven on Jesus.

They came to the house where the child was and saw him with his mother, Mary, and they bowed down and worshiped him. They opened their gifts and gave him treasures of gold, frankincense, and myrrh. (v. 11 NCV)

Behold the first Christian worshippers. The simple dwelling became a cathedral. Seekers of Christ found him and knelt in his presence. They gave him gifts: gold for a king, frankincense for a priest, and myrrh for his burial.

They found the Christ because they heeded the sign and believed the scripture.

Noticeably absent at the manger were the scholars of the Torah. They reported to Herod that the Messiah would be born in Bethlehem. Did they not read the prophecy? Yes, but they did not respond to it. You'd think at a minimum they would have accompanied the magi to Bethlehem. The village was near enough. The risk was small enough. At worst they would be out the effort. At best they would see the fulfillment of prophecy. But the priests showed no interest.

The wise men earned their moniker because they did. Their hearts were open to God's gift. The men were never the same again. After worshiping the Christ child, "they departed for their own country another way" (v. 12 NKJV). Matthew uses the word *way* in other places to suggest a direction of life. He speaks of the narrow way (7:13–14 NASB) and "the way of righteousness" (21:32). He may be telling us that the wise men went home as different men.

Called by a sign. Instructed by Scripture. And directed home by God.

It's as if all the forces of heaven cooperated to guide the wise men.

God uses every possible means to communicate with you. The wonders of nature call to you. The promises and prophecies of Scripture speak to you. God himself reaches out to you. He wants to help you find your way home.

Many years ago I watched the television adaptation of

the drama *The Miracle Worker*, the compelling story of two females with great resolve: Helen Keller and Anne Sullivan. Helen was born in 1880. She wasn't yet two when she contracted an illness that left her blind, deaf, and mute. When Helen was seven years old, Annie, a young, partially blind teacher, came to the Kellers' Alabama home to serve as Helen's teacher.

Helen's brother James tried to convince Annie to quit. The teacher wouldn't consider it. She was resolved to help Helen function in a world of sight and sound. Helen was as stubborn as her teacher. Locked in a frightening, lonely world, she misinterpreted Annie's attempts. The result was a battle of wills. Over and over Annie pressed sign language into Helen's palm. Helen pulled back. Annie persisted. Helen resisted.

Finally, in a moment of high drama, a breakthrough. During a fevered exchange near the water pump, Annie placed one of Helen's hands under the spout of flowing water. Into the other hand she spelled out w-a-t-e-r. Over and over, w-a-t-e-r. Helen pulled back. Annie kept signing. W-a-t-e-r.

All of a sudden Helen stopped. She placed her hand on her teacher's and repeated the letters w-a-t-e-r. Annie beamed. She lifted Helen's hand onto her own cheek and nodded vigorously. "Yes, yes, yes! W-a-t-e-r." Helen spelled it again: w-a-t-e-r. Helen pulled Annie around the yard, spelling out the words. G-r-o-u-n-d. P-o-r-c-h. P-u-m-p. It was a victory parade.[2]

Christmas celebrates a similar moment for us—God breaking through to our world. In a feeding stall of all places. He will not leave us in the dark. He is the pursuer, the teacher. He won't sit back while we miss out. So he entered our world. He sends signals and messages: H-o-p-e. L-i-f-e. He cracks the shell of our world and invites us to peek into his. And every so often a seeking soul looks up.

God will not leave us in the dark. He is the pursuer, the teacher. He won't sit back while we miss out. So he entered our world.

May you be one of them.

When God sends signs, be faithful. Let them lead you to Scripture.

As Scripture directs, be humble. Let it lead you to worship.

And as you worship the Son, be grateful. He will lead you home. Who knows? Perhaps before Jesus comes again, we'll discover why men don't ask for directions. Then we can pursue the other great question of life: Why do women apply makeup while they are driving?

But that's a question for ones wiser than I.

8

Humility Shines

*M*ost of the players in the Christmas drama inspire us with their faith.

Mary, who had great courage.

Joseph, who was obedient.

The shepherds, who came quickly and worshipped willingly.

The wise men, who traveled far and gave generously.

Most of the characters in the Bethlehem drama behaved like heroes. But there was one who played the role of a villain.

Then Herod, when he had secretly called the wise men, determined from them what time the star appeared. And he sent them to Bethlehem and said, "Go and search carefully for the young Child, and when you have found Him, bring back word to me, that I may come and worship Him also." . . .

Then Herod, when he saw that he was deceived by the wise men, was exceedingly angry; and he sent forth and put to death all the male children who were in Bethlehem and in all its districts, from two years old and under, according to the time which he had determined from the wise men. Then was fulfilled what was spoken by Jeremiah the prophet, saying:

"A voice was heard in Ramah,

Lamentation, weeping, and great mourning,

Rachel weeping for her children,

Refusing to be comforted,

Because they are no more." (Matt. 2:7–8, 16–18 NKJV)

Herod and the magi share the same chapter, but they didn't share the same heart. The wise men traveled a great distance to see Jesus. Herod refused to leave his own city. The wise men presented their treasures to honor the child. Herod attempted to kill him. The wise men saw Jesus. But Herod? He saw no one but himself. As a result, his obituary forever contains the sad designation: the first person to reject Jesus Christ.

Dean Farrar, a nineteenth-century British scholar, gave this sobering assessment of the king: "His whole career was red with the blood of murder. . . . Deaths by strangulation, deaths by burning, deaths by being cleft asunder, deaths by secret assassination, confessions forced by unutterable torture, acts of insolent and inhuman lust . . . the survivors during his lifetime were even more miserable than the sufferers."[1]

Herod killed three of his own sons. Caesar Augustus once declared, "It is better to be Herod's hog than his son."[2] What happened to the king? What caused him to commit such violent acts?

Pride. Herod was hooked on his own importance. His arrogance blinded his view of Christ. His ego was threatened the moment he heard the magi's question: "Where is He who has been born King of the Jews?" (Matt. 2:2 NKJV).

Herod was "deeply disturbed by their question" (v. 3 TLB). *King of the Jews? Why, that is my title! That is my assignment!* Under the pretense of interest, Herod asked the temple priests and scholars where the Messiah would be born. When Herod learned the answer, he told the wise men, "Go and search carefully for the young Child, and when you have found Him, bring back word to me, that I may come and worship Him also" (v. 8 NKJV).

He could not bring himself to say, "Search for the king." He could only muster, "Search for the child." He didn't have the integrity to make the three-hour trip or even to send an agent from his court but instead relied on the stargazers to find the child. The wise men did so, yet having been warned in a dream to go home another way, they bypassed Herod on their return trip. Their detour left the megalomaniac livid and bloodthirsty, which resulted in the Bethlehem holocaust.

Just as the same shaft of sunlight in a barn can cause birds to sing and rats to scurry, the same message stirred the worship of the wise men and activated the ire of the king. Herod knew enough to realize that the star and scripture were a forecast of the Messiah, but he used that knowledge to carry out an infanticide. Believing is not obedience, and pride eclipses the right choice from us, even when we know the truth. They say love is blind, but pride is blinder.

Herod's pride hurt other people.

Doesn't it always?

How many apologies has self-importance silenced? How many compliments has arrogance muted? How many broken hearts trace their wounds to someone's stubborn, unyielding, my-way-or-the-highway attitude?

Haughtiness hurts people.

The other day I saw some children at play on a large vacant lot where someone had dumped a mound of dirt. They were playing the greatest of kid games: King of the Mountain. The rules are as simple as they are brutal: fight your way to the top, and shove off anyone who threatens to take your spot. It was a slugfest of crawling, pushing, and falling.

King of the Mountain is not just a kid's game. Versions are played in every dormitory, classroom, boardroom, and bedroom. And since mountaintop real estate is limited, people get shoved around. Mark it down: if you want to be king, someone is going to suffer. Your uppitiness won't prompt a Bethlehem massacre, but it might prompt a broken marriage, an estranged friendship, or a divided office.

Pride comes at a high price.

Don't pay it. Consider the counsel of the apostle Paul: "Do not think of yourself more highly than you ought" (Rom. 12:3).

"How much larger your life would be if your self could become smaller in it," wrote G. K. Chesterton. "You would break out of this tiny and tawdry theatre in which your own little plot is always being played, and you would find yourself under a freer sky."[3]

Some time ago I was honored with a nice recognition. A friend learned about it and said, "Max, God gave you that honor because you were humble enough not to let it go to your head." What kind words! The more I thought about what he had said, the better it felt. The more I thought, the more I agreed. As the day went on, I felt better and better about being so humble. I was proud of my humility. That evening I was just about to tell Denalyn what he had said when I felt a conviction. I was about to brag about being humble!

Humility. The moment you think you have it, you don't.

Pursue it anyway.

A recurring message of Scripture is that God loves the humble heart. Jesus said, "I am gentle and humble in heart" (Matt. 11:29 NASB). "Though the LORD is supreme, he takes care of those who are humble" (Ps. 138:6 NCV). God says, "I . . . live with people who are humble" (Isa. 57:15 GNT). He also says, "These are the ones I look on with favor: those who are humble and contrite" (Isa. 66:2).

And to the humble, God gifts great treasures.

He gives honor: "Humility goes before honor" (Prov. 15:33 NRSV).

To the humble, God gifts great treasures.

He gives wisdom: "With the humble is wisdom" (Prov. 11:2 NKJV).

He gives direction: "He . . . teaches the humble his way" (Ps. 25:9 NRSV).

And most significantly, he gives grace: "God . . . gives grace to the humble" (1 Peter 5:5 NKJV).

And this reassurance: "He crowns the humble with salvation" (Ps. 149:4 WEB).

God loves humility. And by the same token he hates arrogance. He doesn't dislike arrogance. He doesn't disapprove of arrogance. He hates arrogance.

"I hate pride and arrogance" (Prov. 8:13).

"Everyone proud in heart is an abomination to the LORD" (Prov. 16:5 NKJV).

God says, "Do nothing out of . . . vain conceit" (Phil. 2:3) and "Do not let arrogance come out of your mouth" (1 Sam. 2:3 NASB). Just as he gives grace to the humble, "God opposes the proud" (1 Peter 5:5). Just as humility goes before honor, "a proud attitude leads to ruin" (Prov. 16:18 NCV).

Ponder your achievements less; ponder Christ's more. Spend less time on your throne and more at his cross. Brag on his work, not yours. You are valuable, but you aren't invaluable. It is Christ who matters, not us.

Learn a lesson from the sad life of Herod. It's always better to step down from the pedestal than to be pulled off of it. Like the innkeeper, Herod missed an opportunity to see Jesus. God did everything necessary to get Herod's attention. He sent messengers from the East and a message from the Torah. He sent wonders from the sky and words from Scripture. He sent the testimony of the heavens and the teaching of the prophets. But Herod refused to listen. He chose his puny dynasty over Christ.

He died a miserable old man.

Ponder your achievements less;
ponder Christ's more.
Brag on his work, not yours.

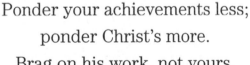

"Realizing how the people disliked him, he ordered his sister Salome and her husband Alexas to slay all the leaders in the hippodrome at the moment of his death, in order to ensure national mourning rather than a festival."[4] The massacre did not occur. His final decree, like his life, proved empty and vain.

Make the wiser choice. The path marked Pride will lead you over a cliff. The path marked Humility will take you to the manger of the Messiah.

9

Perhaps Today

'Tis the season to be looking.
Looking for
   snow if it's cold,
      mistletoe if he's dense,
         instructions if some assembly is required.
Looking for
   red nose lights if you're young,
      headlights if you're a grandma,
         insights if you're a preacher.
            'Tis the season to be looking.

The first Christmas was marked by "lookers" as well. Joseph looked for lodging. Mary looked into the prunish face of Jesus. A thousand angels looked upon the King. The wise men looked at the star. But no one was looking with more intensity than a seasoned saint named Simeon.

Now there was a man in Jerusalem called Simeon, who was righteous and devout. He was waiting for the consolation of Israel, and the Holy Spirit was on him. It had been revealed to him by the Holy Spirit that he would not die before he had seen the Lord's Messiah. Moved by the Spirit, he went into the temple courts. When the parents brought in the child Jesus to do for him what the custom of the Law required, Simeon took him in his arms and praised God, saying:

> "Sovereign Lord, as you have promised,
>> you may now dismiss your servant in peace.
> For my eyes have seen your salvation,
>> which you have prepared in the sight of all nations:
> a light for revelation to the Gentiles,
>> and the glory of your people Israel." (Luke 2:25–32)

Unlike Joseph and Mary, Simeon did not witness Jesus' birth. Unlike the wise men, he did not visit the child in Bethlehem. By the time he saw Jesus, the feeding stall was occupied only by animals, the manger held only hay. Mary and Joseph had caught up on their sleep. The shepherds were back with their sheep.

Forty days had passed. We can know the time with certainty because of the Jewish law. According to the Torah the mother became ceremonially unclean upon the birth of her child.[1] On the eighth day a male baby was circumcised. After an additional thirty-three days, the parents offered a sacrifice (Lev. 12:1–8).

94

A baby dedication of sorts.

It was at this dedication that Simeon saw Jesus.

Simeon was likely an old man—gray haired, white bearded. The years had etched his skin and slowed his step and bent his back. He was waiting for the day when "God would take away Israel's sorrow" (Luke 2:25 NCV). A day in which God would end the alienation of the people and reconcile them to himself.

Simeon knew this day would come in his day. "The Holy Spirit had revealed to him that he would not die until he had seen him—God's anointed King" (v. 26 TLB).

How did the Spirit tell Simeon? In a dream? A vision? A scripture? We don't know. But we do know that Simeon lived with an eye toward the future.

Many years ago I preached a sermon about the return of Christ. I had two words, *Perhaps Today*, printed on a piece of paper and given to the members of the congregation. Recently I was in the home of a member and noticed the sheet, framed and placed in a prominent position.

Simeon would have wanted a copy for his wall. He lived with a "perhaps today" attitude. He knew he would see the Messiah on earth before he saw the Father in heaven. And on the fortieth day after Jesus' birth, the day arrived. "The Spirit led Simeon to the Temple" (v. 27 NCV).

Perhaps he had other plans. Maybe he was going to stay home or visit the grandkids. Perhaps his garden needed watering or the dog needed walking. But then came a nudging, a knowing, a prompting. He decided, *I think I'll go to the temple.*

Simeon wound his way through the narrow streets and over the cobblestone paths. Finally he entered the temple courts. Though Simeon had ascended the temple steps a hundred times, the sight of Herod's masterpiece must have moved him. The massive stones. The gilded roof and great colonnades.[2] Even when it wasn't a holiday, the streets were full of worshippers and pilgrims. Somehow, in spite of the multitude, Simeon spotted Joseph and Mary.

No one else had reason to notice the young parents. Angels did not cast petals or blast trumpets at their arrival. Jesus did not ride on a pillow or in a chariot. He had no halo or glow or aura. He gurgled. He nursed. He slept.

Besides, any passerby had a more important quest. People journeyed to the temple for one reason: to encounter God. No one imagined looking for him in the arms of a simple girl from Nazareth.

No one, that is, except Simeon. "Perhaps today," he whispered to himself as he saw them. He walked briskly across the temple courtyard. He excused his way through the pilgrims and caught up with Joseph. "Pardon me," he said. The Nazarene couple stopped and turned.

Mary's belly was no longer round, but her face was. She had the simple softness of a peasant girl. Joseph wore the scratchy robe of a worker. A year earlier he might have objected to the interruption. But the last few months had been marked by surprises. Angels had spoken and worshipped; shepherds had come and gone. His wife knew childbirth before she knew his bed. Joseph was learning to expect the unexpected. So he tilted his head and waited for Simeon to speak.

And Simeon did. "May I?" He gestured to the child.

The same Spirit that had nudged the older man prompted the younger one, and Joseph nodded. Mary gave Jesus to Simeon, and he "took the baby in his arms and thanked God: 'Now, Lord, you can let me, your servant, die in peace as you said. With my own eyes I have seen your salvation, which you prepared before all people'" (vv. 28–31 NCV).

Simeon's response has come to be known in Latin as *Nunc Dimittis*, or "Now Dismiss."[3] *Now* is a timeline term. It indicates the arrival of a moment. "Now we can go." "Now we can eat." "Now we can start." Simeon saw the arrival of Jesus as a "now" moment, the first day of a new era. Now everything was different. The "consolation of Israel" had begun. The gate of history had swung on the hinge of a Bethlehem gate. The Author of life had turned the page and was ready to write a new chapter.

Simeon did not know the name of the chapter, but we do. Scripture denotes this period as "the last days." Paul said, "In the last days there will be many troubles" (2 Tim. 3:1 NCV). Peter urged us to understand "what will happen in the last days" (2 Peter 3:3 NCV). The author of Hebrews wrote, "But now in these last days God has spoken to us through his Son" (1:2 NCV).

We live between the Advents.

The Second Advent will include the sudden, personal, visible, bodily return of Christ. Jesus promised, "I will come again" (John 14:3 RSV). The author of Hebrews declared, "Christ . . . will appear a second time, not to deal with sin but to save those who are eagerly waiting for him" (9:28 RSV).

As he came, Christ will come. But he won't come *as* he came.

He came quietly in Bethlehem. He will return in glory with a shout. "All who are in their graves will hear his voice and come out" (John 5:28–29).

In Bethlehem, Joseph placed Jesus in a manger. At his return Jesus will be seated on a throne.

In Bethlehem the just-born Jesus slept. When he returns, "the Lord himself will come down from heaven, with a loud command, with the voice of the archangel and with the trumpet call of God" (1 Thess. 4:16).

At his first coming few noticed. At his second "all the nations of the world will be gathered before him" (Matt. 25:32 NCV).

In Bethlehem, Joseph placed Jesus in a manger. At his return Jesus will be seated on a throne: "The Son of Man will come again in his great glory, with all his angels. He will be King and sit on his great throne" (Matt. 25:31 NCV).

"*What will happen next*, and what we hope for, is what God promised: a new heaven and a new earth where justice reigns" (2 Peter 3:13 *The Voice*). History is not an endless succession of meaningless circles but a directed movement toward a great event. God has a timeline. And because of Bethlehem, we have an idea where we stand on it. As the apostle John said, "My dear children, these are the last days" (1 John 2:18 NCV). We enjoy the fruit of the first coming but anticipate the glory of the second. We refuse to believe that this present world is the sum total of human existence. We celebrate the First Advent to whet our appetites for the Second. We long for the next coming.

God has a timeline. And because
of Bethlehem, we have an idea
where we stand on it.

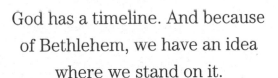

I found a metaphor for this longing in the West Texas oil fields. My father thought Christmas break was an opportunity for his son to make some good cash. Anyone who could dig a ditch and endure the cold wind would make money.

So as a teenager I spent many a December day in the vast flatlands of the Permian Basin.

The routine was simple. A foreman would drive a truck full of workers to the edge of civilization and show us the ditch that had been dug with a large machine. The furrow was about six feet deep. Before pipe could be placed inside it, the excess rocks and dirt needed to be removed. He would say, "Get to work. I'll come back for you." And then he would drive off.

A root canal would have been more pleasant. Nothing blocks the cold prairie wind in December. It chills the bone. We were miles from another human being. A person can see forever out there. If only there were something to see! We had nothing to do but dig, so we did. All day. By midafternoon we began thinking, *Maybe the foreman's on his way.*

By four o'clock our backs would be tired. We'd lift our heads from the ditch and sweep the horizon. "Does anyone see him?"

By five o'clock we were digging, then looking, digging, then looking.

By sunset, when the already-cold air would turn icy, we would begin to encourage one another with words like "He'll be here soon." We'd think about the dinner that awaited us. The warm house, the hot bath. And just when we thought we couldn't wait any longer, a set of familiar headlights would come bouncing over the horizon. No one had to tell us to climb out of the ditch and gather our tools.

We were ready when he came to take us home.

Some of you have been digging a long time. You're tired from the toil. The ditch is deep, and the work seems endless. You carry the burden of a broken heart. You've walked a long, lonely road. The wind is a cold one, and the world seems as barren as a prairie. You have searched the horizon for the coming of the King. You're wondering, *Is he really coming for us?*

Your wait is nearly over. If all of history were but a year, the leaves would now be autumn gold.

If all of history were merely a day, the sun would have begun to set.

If all of history were just an hour, the minute hands of the clock would be nearing full circle.

Some people say they know the day and the hour of his return. I don't. But I do know the Bible urges us to look for specific signs that point to the return of Christ.

- The preaching of the gospel to all nations (Matt. 24:14; Mark 13:10)
- Days of distress in which saints will suffer and the creation will tremble (Mark 13:7–8, 19–20)
- The coming of the Antichrist, an enemy of God who will deceive many (2 Thess. 2:1–10)
- Salvation of many Jews (Rom. 11:12, 25–26)
- Signs in the heavens (Mark 13:24–25)
- False prophets (Mark 13:22)

To a certain degree each of these signs has seen ful-fillment. The gospel has gone around the world. Many Christians experience severe oppression. The world has suffered at the hands of global villains. Many Jews have been saved. Our earth has shaken from birth pangs, and the church has been weakened by false prophets.

Certainly, these signs will see further fulfillment. But this much is sure: the end is near. Or, better said, the *beginning* is near.

> Lo, the days are hastening on
> By prophets seen of old.
> When with the ever circling years
> Shall come the time foretold.
> When peace shall over all the earth
> Its ancient splendors fling.
> And the whole world give back the song
> Which now the angels sing.[4]

'Tis the season to be looking not for a jolly man in a red suit but for a grand King on a white horse. At his command the sea will give up the dead, the Devil will give up his quest, kings and queens will give up their crowns, broken hearts will give up their despair, and God's children will lift up their worship. Wise is the saint who searches like Simeon. If you knew Jesus was returning tomorrow, how would you feel today? Anxious, afraid, unprepared? If so, you can take care of your fears by placing your trust in Christ. If your answer includes words like *happy*, *relieved*, and *excited*, hold tightly to your joy. Heaven is God's answer to any suffering you may face.

If you knew Jesus was coming tomorrow, what would you do today? Then do it! Live in such a way that you would not have to change your plans.

In an earlier chapter I mentioned the sorrow that plagued our family one December. Our daughter suffered a miscarriage during the Advent season. The next year, however, the sorrow was replaced with joy. Christmas brought the excitement of her healthy pregnancy. So healthy, in fact, that Jenna gave each of us an assignment. She was at the point in her pregnancy when the baby was developing the ability to hear. So she asked family members to record audio messages that she could play for her yet-to-be-born daughter.

Who could refuse such an opportunity? I retreated to a quiet corner and captured this welcome.

Dear, dear child. We are so excited to welcome you into the world. We are waiting for you. Your parents have prepared a place for you. You have grandparents, aunts, and uncles ready to shower you with love. We cannot wait to spend time loving you and showing you your wonderful new home.

Only after I finished did I realize that is God's invitation to us! He has prepared a place. He has a family to love us. And he has a sparkling new world to show us. Who knows? This could be the day of our delivery.

10

Crown, Cradle, and Cross

The large box sat unexplained in the corner of our living room for weeks. It appeared soon after Thanksgiving and sat untouched throughout most of December. It was as tall as I was, which isn't saying much. I was only four years old. Unlike the other boxes near the Christmas tree, this one bore no glistening wrapping paper or shiny ribbons. It displayed no name, neither of giver nor receiver. It was taped shut, tightly shut, or my brother and I would have opened it. All we could do was ask about it.

Mom had no explanation. She seemed unimpressed. "Just something your dad bought for Christmas." If anything, she assumed Dad had used Christmas as an excuse to buy himself a gift. He'd always wanted an outboard motor to mount on a fishing boat. Did the box contain one?

On Christmas morning while my older sisters opened gifts and my brother and I scampered about playing with our new toys, my mom noticed the still-unopened gorilla of a box.

"Jack," she said, "aren't you going to open the big present?"

Dad could no more keep a straight face than he could walk to the moon on a moonbeam. He began to smile, his eyebrows arched like little rainbows, and he looked at her with a Santa sort of twinkle. "That gift isn't for me; it's for you."

My brother and I stopped and looked. Dad winked at us. We looked at Mom. She was looking at Dad. We knew something fun was about to happen. Mom stepped toward the box. Dad grabbed the 8-millimeter camera, and we kids scurried over.

Mom pried open the top of the nondescript, unaddressed box. She reached in and pulled out nothing but tissue paper. One armful after another.

A remarkable gift can arrive
in an unremarkable package.
One did in Bethlehem.

The image in the film, which our family later loved to watch, rewind, and watch again, begins to shake as Dad begins to giggle. "Keep digging, Thelma," he says from behind the camera.

"What's in here?" she asks, still pulling out paper. Finally she strikes pay dirt. A box within the box. She opens it to find another box. She opens it, then another. This happens a couple more times until at last she reaches the smallest of the boxes. A ring box. My brother and I shout, "Open it, Mom!" She smiles at the camera. "Jack."

I didn't understand the romantic significance of a new ring. But I did learn a lesson: a remarkable gift can arrive in an unremarkable package. One did in the Lucado house.

One did in Bethlehem.

No one expected God to come the way he did. Yet the way he came was every bit as important as the coming itself. The manger is the message. At least this was the opinion of the apostle Paul.

Paul. His name seldom appears in Christmas reflections. We typically think of Joseph, Mary, the shepherds, and the magi. We don't often refer to the reformed Pharisee. Yet we should. His words are the Bible's most eloquent summary of the Bethlehem promise. The descended Christ is now the ascended Christ, and he reigns over us.

In your relationships with one another, have the same mindset as Christ Jesus:

> Who, being in very nature God,
>   did not consider equality with God something
>   to be used to his own advantage;
> rather, he made himself nothing

by taking the very nature of a servant,
being made in human likeness.
And being found in appearance as a man,
he humbled himself
by becoming obedient to death—even death on
a cross!

Therefore God exalted him to the highest place
and gave him the name that is above every name,
that at the name of Jesus every knee should bow,
in heaven and on earth and under the earth,
and every tongue acknowledge that Jesus Christ
is Lord,
to the glory of God the Father. (Phil. 2:5–11)

The apostle was not writing a Christmas sermon. His aim was far more mundane. Paul was counseling a church. The Christians in Philippi seemed to have a few issues, selfish ambition and conceit being among them (2:3). Later in his letter he mentions two women, Euodia and Syntyche. They couldn't get along. Paul was urging them to "be of the same mind in the Lord" (4:2). Paul was appealing to the church to seek humility. As a result we have this fourchapter letter. In the heart of the epistle is the heart of the gospel. A six-verse summary of God's divine intervention. Some scholars think the text is a hymn. If so, then the words compose one of the earliest Christian hymns. Others describe the pericope as a liturgy that was read in the first churches. Still others believe the passage was originally a poem. I like that thought: Paul the poet laureate of Advent. Whether it is a hymn, a liturgy, or a poem from the pen of the apostle, we know this: the reading is eloquent.

Jesus was "in very nature God." Before Bethlehem, Jesus had every advantage and benefit of deity. He was boundless, timeless, and limitless. "All things were made through Him, and without Him nothing was made that was made" (John 1:3 NKJV).

Every rock, tree, and planet needs a stamp that says "Made by Jesus." He gets credit for the Whirlpool Galaxy. It contains more than a hundred billion stars.[1] He created our sun. More than a million Earths could fit inside the sun.[2] Jesus fashioned Betelgeuse, which if it were placed at the center of the Earth's solar system would extend out to the orbit of Jupiter.[3] The star Betelgeuse is approximately a thousand times bigger than our sun.[4] Jesus spoke and the bespangled sky happened. He calls each star by name and can fold up the skies as a bedouin would pack his tent.

Paul's headline, however, is not "Christ the Creator"; it is "Christ the Incarnate One." The One who made everything "made himself nothing." Christ made himself small. He made himself dependent upon lungs, a larynx, and legs. He experienced hunger and thirst. He went through all the normal stages of human development. He was taught to walk, stand, wash his face, and dress himself. His muscles grew stronger; his hair grew longer. His voice cracked when he passed through puberty. He was genuinely human.

When he was "full of joy" (Luke 10:21), his joy was authentic. When he wept for Jerusalem (Luke 19:41), his tears were as real as yours or mine. When he asked, "How long must I put up with you?" (Matt. 17:17 NLT), his frustration was honest. When he cried out from the cross, "My God, my God, why have you forsaken me?" (Matt. 27:46), he needed an answer. He knew only what the Father revealed to him (John 12:50). If the Father did not give direction, Jesus did not claim to have it.

He took "the very nature of a servant" (Phil. 2:7). He became like us so he could serve us! He entered the world not to demand our allegiance but to display his affection.

He entered the world not to demand our allegiance but to display his affection.

Jesus did not view his equality with God as "something to be grasped" (Phil. 2:6 NET) or "exploited" (NRSV). He refused to throw his weight around. He divested himself of divine advantage.

When people mocked him, he didn't turn them into stones. When soldiers spat on him, he didn't boomerang their spit. When people called him crazy, he didn't strike them blind. Just the opposite. He became "obedient to death—even death on a cross!" (v. 8).

Paul gave special emphasis: "*even* death on a cross" (emphasis mine). Crucifixion was the cruelest form of execution in the Roman Empire. It was commonly reserved for those of the lowest class, especially slaves. It was regulated only by the morality of the executioners, and they had little to speak of. The victim was tortured, whipped, nailed to a beam of wood, and impaled with a spear. He was left naked and bloody, suspended for all to see. He became a public example of how society treats evildoers.

It cannot be said too often that was God on that cross. *God* took the nails. *God* took the whips. *God* bore the shame. *God* felt the tip of the spear. *God* exhaled a final breath.

Jesus descended the ladder of incarnation one rung at a time.

In nature, God.

He did not grasp equality with God.

He made himself nothing.

He took on the form of a servant.

He submitted himself to death.

Even death on a cross.

Down, down, down, down. From heaven's crown to Bethlehem's cradle to Jerusalem's cross.

It was one thing for Christ to enter a womb, quite another for him to be placed in a tomb. But the tomb could not hold him. Paul's poem takes on a triumphant tone. "Therefore God exalted him to the highest place and gave him the name that is above every name" (v. 9).

The One who went low is now made high. The One who descended is now exalted. Jesus is promoted to the "highest place." No angel is higher. No political office is higher. Jesus outranks every ruler and conqueror. Jesus is, right now, in the highest place. He occupies the only true throne in the universe. Every other throne is made of papier-mâché and is doomed to pass. Not the throne of Jesus. God "gave him the name that is above every name" (v. 9).

Names carry clout. When the name *Queen Elizabeth* is announced, people turn. When the letter is signed by John F. Kennedy, it is treasured and stored in a safe-deposit box. Napoleon, Caesar, Alexander the Great—all these names turned heads. But only one name will forever cause them to bow: "At the name of Jesus every knee should bow, in heaven and on earth and under the earth" (v. 10).

The poor. The rich. The black. The brown. The politician. The physician. The red-carpet superstar. The street-corner panhandler. Every knee will bow before Jesus. And "every tongue will confess that Jesus Christ is Lord" (v. 11 NASB).

There are people on our planet who mock the name of Jesus. They scoff at the idea of God on earth. They renounce their need for a Savior and cast aspersions on any who believe in Christ. They are self-sufficient, independent, self-made, and self-reliant. Ask them to bend a knee before

Jesus, and they will laugh at you. But they will not laugh forever. A day is coming in which they will bow in his presence. Stalin will confess his name. Herod will confess his name. Even, or especially, Satan will confess his name. "All who have raged against him will come to him and be put to shame" (Isa. 45:24).

One ruler after another will step forward. Crowns will be collected at the foot of Jesus' throne. So will Pulitzers, Nobels, and gold medals. MVP? PhD? MD? All recognitions will become instantly puny in the presence of Christ the Creator. No one will boast. All the money in history will be shown to be counterfeit. Every Rolls-Royce will seem to be an oxcart. Nothing will matter. No one will matter.

Just Jesus.

On the Great Day you'll hear billions of voices make the identical claim about Jesus Christ. Multitudes of people will bow low like a field of wheat blown by the wind, each one saying to Jesus, "You are the Christ, the Son of the living God" (Matt. 16:16 NKJV).

Those who worshipped him on earth will confess him gladly. Those who didn't will confess him regretfully. Believers will receive their inheritance. Unbelievers will receive theirs: separation from Christ.

In one of his broadcasts C. S. Lewis stated:

God will invade . . . When that happens, it's the end of the world. When the author walks on to the stage the play's over . . . For this time it will be God *without* disguise; something so overwhelming that it will strike either irresistible love or irresistible horror into every creature. It will be too late then to *choose* your side . . . It will be the time when we discover which side we really have chosen.[5]

By the way, Jesus has not surrendered his earthly body. The incarnation that began in Bethlehem continues at this moment in the heavens. When Jesus ascended, he did so in a human body. Having become a man, he will never cease to be a man. The God-in-the-flesh remains exactly that!

Why does this matter? There is a human being in charge of the universe. Glorified, for sure. Exalted, by all means. Utterly divine, certainly. But still, the hand that directs the affairs of humanity is the same hand that held a hammer in Nazareth. In the center of that hand is a scar, an eternal reminder of God's eternal love.

Humble yourself before the One who humbled himself for you.

Bow before him. Humble yourself before the One who humbled himself for you.

And to think, it all began in the most inconspicuous of places: a hay box in Bethlehem.

11

It's Good-Bye to the Bents

The Christmas tree hunt is on. Families are entering tents and patrolling sidewalks. They lift limbs and examine needles. They measure. They ponder. They consider. They barter.

The tree can't be too tall or too short. It needs to fit the room and the budget. It must be full yet not dense, mature but not dry. A noble fir for some. A Douglas fir or Virginia pine for others. The preferences are different, but the desire is the same. We want the perfect Christmas tree.

And, oh, the special moment when we find it. When we lash it to the car. Drag it into the house and set it in the tree stand.

We revel in this moment. Only a few people have won the U.S. Open, completed an Ironman triathlon, or qualified as Rhodes Scholars. Fewer still have positioned a Christmas tree so that it doesn't lean.

Throughout the year we prepare. We read articles, attend seminars, swap ideas, and share secrets. We are bonded by the desire to avoid the tragedy of the holiday season: a leaning tree.

One year I barely escaped. Denalyn and I placed the tree in the stand, stood back, and sighed at what we saw. The dreaded tilt. I crawled under the branches and began adjusting the screws until the tree stood as straight as a stalk of wheat. We stepped back and admired my engineering skills. Denalyn placed her arm in mine, and I choked back tears of joy. My children called me blessed. Angels began to sing. The blast of trumpets sounded in the front yard, where neighbors had gathered. The White House called to congratulate me. We strung the lights and hung the decorations. It was a wonderful night.

Then disaster struck. The tree started to lean again. Decorations shook, lights shifted, Denalyn shouted, and I ran to the rescue.

This time I placed the tree on its side, removed the stand, and saw the root of the problem. Just six inches above the cut line was a right turn. Our tree was crooked! Once upon a time in a forest, this tree had been a leaner! And now here it was, in our house, in broad daylight, in front of my own children—leaning again!

What's a person to do? As I was retrieving a saw from the garage, it occurred to me: I'm not the first father to deal with this issue. God faces this situation on a continual basis. Don't we have our share of unattractive bents?

I know I do. Take just the last three days:

- I avoided returning a call to a congregant because most of the time conversations with him generate more whine than Napa Valley. I saw his number on my phone and groaned, "I don't want an earful of his woes." And I'm a pastor! One of his pastors! I'm supposed to love the sheep, feed the sheep, and care for the sheep. And I avoided this sheep. (I eventually called. He wanted to compliment a sermon.)

- I woke up at 2:30 yesterday morning, reliving the outcome of a meeting. I disagreed with a particular decision. When the vote was taken, I was in the minority. And I was ticked off. Between 2:30 a.m. and 3:30 a.m., I convicted each of the other team members of stupidity and insensitivity. My thought pattern was toxic.

- And then there is the issue of a deadline. Will I make it? Why did I agree to it? Why does the publisher demand it? Don't they know it takes space for a fragile soul like mine to create?

Would that I stood as straight as a sequoia, but I don't. And since I don't, I find a kindred spirit in the Christmas tree. I think you will find the same. What you do for a tree, God does for you.

He picked you.

Do you purchase the first tree you see? Of course not. You search for the right one. You walk the rows. You lift several up and set them down. You examine them from all angles until you decide, *This one is perfect.* You have a place in mind where the tree will sit. Not just any tree will do.

God does the same. He knows just the place where you'll be placed. He has a barren living room in desperate need of warmth and joy. A corner of the world needs some color. He selected you with that place in mind.

As King David wrote, "You made my whole being; you formed me in my mother's body. I praise you because you made me in an amazing and wonderful way. What you have done is wonderful. . . . All the days planned for me were written in your book before I was one day old" (Ps. 139:13–14, 16 NCV).

God made you on purpose with a purpose. He interwove calendar and character, circumstance and personality to create the right person for the right corner of the world, and then he paid the price to take you home.

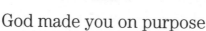

God made you on purpose
with a purpose.

He purchased you.

We don't ask the tree-lot owner to give us the tree for free. The kid who loads the tree in the trunk doesn't shell out the cash; we do. We make the necessary payment.

God did the same. "God bought you with a high price" (1 Cor. 6:20 NLT).

Rick Warren tells about a time he was sitting in a parking lot. His three-year-old daughter was in the backseat in her car seat. As they waited for his wife to come out of the store, his daughter grew restless. Anticipating a short wait, Rick didn't want to remove her. The little girl hung her head out the window and yelled, "Please, God! Get me out of this!"[1]

At some point in life, don't we all feel like Rick's daughter? We are stuck. Not stuck in a backseat, but stuck in a dying body, with bad habits, suffering the consequences of poor choices in a rebellious world. We need help.

So we shop till we drop, drink till we can't think, work till we can't stop. We do anything possible to get our minds off our mess, only to wake up, sober up, or sit up and realize we are still stuck.

So we take pills, take vacations, and take advice from therapists, bartenders, and big brothers. We buy new purses or Porsches. We change hair color, lovers, and the shape of our tummies. But we end up facing the same mess.

We need someone to save us from meaninglessness and meanness. We are lost and need to be found and taken home. We need a Savior. The Christmas promise is this: we have a Savior, and his name is Jesus.

His time on earth was a search-and-rescue mission. He rescued a woman hiding in Samaria. Five husbands had dumped her like the morning garbage. The sixth wouldn't marry her. She was the town scamp. She filled her water bucket in the heat of the day to avoid the stares of the people. Christ went out of his way to help her.[2]

The Christmas promise is this: we have a Savior, and his name is Jesus.

He rescued a demoniac in the caves. Evil spirits had driven the man to mutilate himself, slashing himself with stones. One word from Christ stopped the hurting.[3]

He spotted pint-size Zacchaeus in Jericho. The tax collector had swindled enough people to stockpile his retirement. Yet he would have given it all for a clean conscience and a good friend. One lunch with Jesus and he found both.[4]

Jesus' ministry went on like this for three years. He changed person after person; no one quite knew how to respond to this carpenter who commanded the dead. His healing hands had calluses; his divine voice had an accent. He tended to doze off on boats and grow hungry on trips. Yet he scared the hell out of the possessed and gave hope to the dispossessed. Just when he seemed poised for a crown, he died on a cross.

We don't know why the cross of Christ is often called a tree. Perhaps the earliest crosses were actually trees. Or since crosses were formed from trees, maybe the name stuck. But whatever the reason, the first-century writers often called the cross a tree. Peter did when he declared, "[Jesus] Himself bore our sins in His own body on the tree" (1 Peter 2:24 NKJV).

Somewhere on the timeline between the Tree of Knowledge in the garden and the Tree of Life in heaven is the Tree of Sacrifice near Jerusalem. And if Christmas trees are known for beauty and gifts, then who would deny that the most wonderful Christmas tree was a rugged one on a bald knob? "God . . . loved us and sent His *unique* Son *on a special mission* to become an atoning sacrifice for our sins" (1 John 4:10 *The Voice*). Jesus took on our sin. He was covered by the rebellion that separated us from God. He endured what we should have endured. He paid the price to save us.

When we were still powerless, Christ died for the ungodly. (Rom. 5:6)

Christ . . . died for sins once for all, the righteous for the unrighteous, that he might bring us to God. (1 Peter 3:18 RSV)

In the manger God loves you; through the cross God saves you. But has he taken you to his home? Not yet. He has work for you to do. He wants the world to see what God can do with his purchased possessions.

So . . . he prunes you.

He takes an ax to your prejudices and clippers to your self-pity, and when there is a tilt in your character that needs to be removed, he's been known to pull out the old Black & Decker. Jesus said, "My Father is the gardener. . . . He trims and cleans every branch that produces fruit so that it will produce even more fruit" (John 15:1–2 NCV).

In the manger God loves you; through the cross God saves you.

Once he stabilizes us, the decorating begins. He festoons us with the fruit of the Spirit: love, joy, peace, patience, kindness, goodness, faithfulness, gentleness, and self-control (Gal. 5:22–23 NCV). He crowns us. Most people crown their Christmas trees with either an angel or a star. God uses both. He sends his angels to protect us and his Word as a star to guide us.

Then he surrounds us with his grace. We become his depot, the distribution point of God's gifts. He wants no one to leave our presence empty-handed. Some people find the gift of salvation. For others the gifts are smaller: a kind word, a good deed. But all the gifts are from God.

Our task is to stand tall in his love, secure in our place, sparkling in kindness, surrounded by his goodness, freely giving to all who come our way.

You, me, and the Christmas tree. Picked, purchased, and pruned. Trust God's work.

You, me, and the Christmas tree. Picked, purchased, and pruned.

Trust God's work.

You're going to look much better without the bents.

12

---⊗⊗⊗---

Every Day a Christmas, Every Heart a Manger

Hollywood would recast the Christmas story. Joseph's collar is way too blue. Mary is green from inexperience. The couple's star power doesn't match the bill. Too obscure. Too simple. The story warrants some headliners. A square-jawed Joseph. Someone of the Clooney vintage. And Mary needs a beauty mark and glistening teeth. Angelina Jolie–ish. And what about the shepherds? Do they sing? If so, perhaps Bono and U2?

Hollywood would recast the story.

A civilized person would sanitize it. No person, however poor, should be born in a cow stall. Hay on the floor. Animals on the hay. Don't place the baby in a feed trough; the donkey's nose has been there. Don't wrap the newborn in rags. They smell like sheep. Speaking of smells, watch where you step.

A good public-relations firm would move the birth to a big city. See what Roman palaces they might rent, what Greek villas they could lease. The Son of God deserves a royal entry. Less peasant, more pizzazz. Out with the heads of sheep, in with the heads of state. Shouldn't we ticker tape this event? You'd think so.

Let stallions prance and trumpets blast. Summon emperors from ancient thrones and palaces not yet built. Abraham and Moses should kneel at the manger. Even Adam and Eve should come to Bethlehem and bow before the Alpha and the Omega, whom Mary holds.

But we didn't design the hour. God did. And God was content to enter the world in the presence of sleepy sheep and a wide-eyed carpenter. No spotlights, just candlelight. No crowns, just cows chewing cud.

God made so little of his Son's coming. He didn't even circle the date on the calendar. Ancient Christmases bounced from date to date before landing on December 25. Some early leaders favored dates in March. For centuries the Eastern Orthodox church celebrated Christmas on January 6, and some still do. Only in the fourth century did the church choose December 25 as the date to celebrate Jesus' coming.[1] We've made bigger deals out of lesser comings. How could this be? No exact date of birth. No hoopla at his birth. Is this a mistake?

Or is this the message?

Maybe your life resembles a Bethlehem stable. Crude in some spots, smelly in others. Not much glamour. Not always neat. People in your circle remind you of stable animals: grazing like sheep, stubborn like donkeys, and that cow in the corner looks a lot like the fellow next door.

You, like Joseph, knocked on the innkeeper's door. But you were too late. Or too old, sick, dull, damaged, poor, or peculiar. You know the sound of a slamming door. So here you are in the grotto, always on the outskirts of activity, it seems.

You do your best to make the best of it, but try as you might, the roof still leaks, and the winter wind still sneaks through the holes you just can't seem to fix. You've shivered through your share of cold nights.

And you wonder if God has a place for a person like you. Find your answer in the Bethlehem stable.

If you wonder if God has a place for a person like you, find your answer in the Bethlehem stable.

Imagine two angels on a tour of the universe, as J. B. Phillips did. His Christmas analogy casts light on God's love. The angels fly from galaxy to galaxy until they enter the one in which we live. As the sun and its orbiting planets come into view, the senior angel calls attention to a somewhat smaller member of the solar system.

"I want you to watch that one particularly," said the senior angel, pointing with his finger.

"Well, it looks very small and rather dirty to me," said the little angel. "What's special about that one?"

His superior explained that the unimpressive ball was the renowned Visited Planet. The lesser angel was surprised.

"Do you mean that our great and glorious Prince . . . went down in Person to this fifth-rate little ball? . . .

"Do you mean to tell me," he said, "that He stooped so low as to become one of those creeping, crawling creatures of that floating ball?"

"I do, and I don't think He would like you to call them 'creeping, crawling creatures' in that tone of voice. For, strange as it may seem to us, He loves them. He went down to visit them to lift them up to become like Him."[2]

It really comes down to that: God loves us. The story of Christmas is the story of God's relentless love for us.

The story of Christmas is the story of God's relentless love for us.

Let him love you. If God was willing to wrap himself in rags and drink from a mother's breast, then all questions about his love for you are off the table. You might question his actions, decisions, or declarations. But you can never, ever question his zany, stunning, unquenchable affection.

The moment Mary touched God's face is the moment God made his case: there is no place he will not go. If he is willing to be born in a barnyard, then expect him to be at work anywhere—bars, bedrooms, boardrooms, and brothels. No place is too common. No person is too hardened. No distance is too far. There is no person he cannot reach. There is no limit to his love.

When Christ was born, so was our hope.

When Christ was born, so was our hope.

This is why I love Christmas. The event invites us to believe the wildest of promises: God became one of us so we could become one with him. He did away with every barrier, fence, sin, bent, debt, and grave. Anything that might keep us from him was demolished. He only awaits our word to walk through the door.

Invite him in. Escort him to the seat of honor, and pull out his chair. Clear the table; clear the calendar. Call the kids and neighbors.

Christmas is here. Christ is here.

One request from you, and God will do again what he

did then: scatter the night with everlasting light. He'll be born in you.

Listen as God whispers, "No mess turns me back; no smell turns me off. I live to live in a life like yours. Every heart can be a manger. Every day can be a Christmas. Let 'Silent Night' be sung on summer nights. Let Advent brighten the autumn chill. The Christmas miracle is a year-long celebration."

May this prayer be yours:

My Heart, Your Manger

Like the stable in which you lay,
my heart is simple, frail as hay.
But if you would within me stay,
Make my heart your manger, I pray.
Make my world your Bethlehem,
centerpieced with heaven's Son.
Make this night a shepherd's sky,
quickened bright with holy dawn.
Rush the air with cherub wings.
Brush this earth. Let angels sing.
A glimpse of your face. A taste of your grace.
Be born in this place.
I pray.
Amen

BECAUSE OF

Bethlehem

Advent Devotional Guide

Prepared by Christine Anderson

$\mathcal{E}$very year Advent invites us to prepare our hearts once more for the gift—the gift that seemingly is too good to be true but is, in fact, miraculously and joyously true! And each year, we have the opportunity to say yes to that invitation, to prepare our hearts for the miracle of Immanuel, "God with us."

The word *advent* comes from the Latin word *adventus* and simply means "coming" or "arrival." Advent begins each year on the fourth Sunday before Christmas, which is the Sunday closest to November 30. It is a season in which Christians around the world celebrate the First Advent, Jesus' birth, and also anticipate the Second Advent, Christ's return. Although the themes of Advent sometimes vary, those most commonly observed during the four weeks of Advent are hope, peace, joy, and love.

This guide has five devotions—one for each of the four weeks of Advent and one for Christmas Eve/Christmas Day. Each devotion includes the following:

- *Scripture.* Passages traditionally read during Advent are taken from both the Old and New Testaments, and include selections from the Psalms, the Prophets, the Epistles, and the Gospels.
- *Questions for Reflection.* Drawing on the themes of Scripture and related passages from *Because of Bethlehem*, the questions are designed to help you explore the intersection between your life and the Advent theme for each week.
- *Advent Prayer.* You can tuck these brief and simple prayers into your pocket and take them with you wherever you go. Pray them often to bring the promise of each week's theme into every circumstance you encounter.
- *Advent Practice.* Practices provide a way to explore and to respond to what you learn. Each week includes options to help deepen your experience of that week's theme.

As you reflect on the miracle of Christ's birth and the promise of his return, may you experience the true meaning of Christmas: Immanuel, God with us—*God with you.*

Week 1: Hope

—⊷⊶—

The manger dares us to believe the best is
yet to be. And it could all begin today.

At Advent, we are invited to immerse ourselves
in hope. Biblical hope is not wishful thinking. It
is the unshakable confidence that God can be trusted. It is
the belief that God is always at work for our good (Rom.
8:24–25, 28). It is the assurance that God's promises are
true even while we wait for their fulfillment. Because our
hope is certain, we wait patiently, not fretfully, trusting that
God is already at work to provide the light we seek, the help
we need, and the deliverance we long for.

Scripture
Psalm 80:1–7, 17–19
Isaiah 2:1–5
Romans 13:11–14
Mark 13:24–37

Questions for Reflection

1. Advent is the season to be looking—looking for light, for rescue, for every promised good thing. Each of these Scripture passages reflects some aspect of this eager and hopeful anticipation. The psalmist implored God, "Let your face shine, that we may be saved" (Ps. 80:3 NRSV). The prophet Isaiah charged God's people to "walk in the light of the LORD!" (Isa. 2:5 NRSV). The apostle Paul roused his readers with the command, "Wake from sleep . . . and put on the armor of light" (Rom. 13:11–12 NRSV). And Jesus urged his followers to "keep alert . . . keep awake" (Mark 13:33, 35 NRSV).

   - Which of these four directives from Scripture resonates most with you right now? Why?
   - The emphases on light and alertness indirectly acknowledge other, less-welcome realities, such as darkness, danger, lethargy, and exhaustion. As you anticipate the weeks leading up to Christmas, what unwelcome realities could you be facing?
   - The answer to darkness is light, to danger is rescue, to lethargy is vitality, to exhaustion is rest. Which of

these do you think you will need most in the days and weeks ahead?

2. The prophet Isaiah described an expansive vision of what will happen when the hope of the coming Messiah is realized: nations "will beat their swords into plowshares and their spears into pruning hooks. Nation will not take up sword against nation, nor will they train for war anymore" (Isa. 2:4). When the Messiah reigns, warriors become farm workers, soldiers grow vegetables, and troopers till the soil.

   - In what ways does the holiday season (or the stress of everyday life) bring out the fight in you—your warrior/soldier/trooper instincts? What are your weapons of choice, your equivalent of swords and spears?

   - If the Messiah is to reign in your life this Advent and Christmas, in what situations or relationships might you need to lay down your arms? What are your equivalents of plowshares and pruning hooks? Or how might you exchange your weapons for the "armor of light" (Rom. 13:12)?

3. At Advent hope fills us with anticipation—the King is coming and we want everything in our lives to be ready to receive him! Max puts it this way: "If you knew Jesus was coming tomorrow, what would you do today? Then do it! Live in such a way that you would not have to change your plans" (page 103).

- Allow yourself to imagine that Jesus will make a literal visit to your home and that you have four weeks to get ready. If you want to be at your best and to fully enjoy the visit, how would you prepare?

  I would prepare physically by . . .

  I would prepare relationally by . . .

  I would prepare emotionally by . . .

  I would prepare financially by . . .

  I would prepare spiritually by . . .

- In what ways, if any, would you need to reorder your life or schedule to make this preparation? What would move up on your priority list, and what would move down?

- The culture in Jesus' day placed a very high value on hospitality. Among other things, welcoming an honored guest might include greeting the person with a kiss, pouring oil on the head, and providing water to wash the feet (Luke 7:44–46). Together these gestures created a warm welcome so guests felt not only refreshed and respected but also genuinely wanted and appreciated. What comes to mind when you consider welcoming Jesus in a way that would make him feel not just respected or worshipped but genuinely wanted and appreciated? In what ways, if any, would it change your preparations?

4. Max writes, "The manger . . . dares us to believe the best is yet to be. And it could all begin today" (page 9).

If Advent and Christmas were everything you could hope for this year, what words or phrases would you use to describe them?

Advent Prayer

Come, Lord Jesus. My hope is in you.

Advent Practice

Consider using one or more of the following options to help you practice and experience hope this week.

- Train your heart to seek the light of Christ by noticing all the lights around you throughout the day—everything from sunrise to holiday lights to the little light at the back of the refrigerator. Stuck in rush-hour traffic? Let the brake lights on the car in front of you prompt you to use your Advent Prayer, *Come, Lord Jesus. My hope is in you.* If you find it helpful, keep a daily light list or use your phone to take pictures of all the lights that prompt you to invite the light and hope of Christ into each moment of your day.
- Set aside time for preparation. Briefly review your responses to question 3, and follow through on one or more of the preparations you identified. For example, *I would prepare physically by getting eight hours of sleep each night.* Then work through your schedule for the week(s) ahead, making any necessary changes so you

can prepare for, receive, and truly enjoy the coming of Christ.

- Make or buy a simple Advent wreath to mark the progression of Advent from week to week. Light the appropriate candle(s) each Sunday. You may also choose to relight them when you pray each day or when you have your evening meals as a reminder that the light of Christ is always with you. If this hasn't been a tradition in your home, now is a good time to begin an annual Advent tradition with your family.

Advent Hymn

O LITTLE TOWN OF BETHLEHEM

O little town of Bethlehem, how still we see thee lie!
Above thy deep and dreamless sleep the silent stars go by;
Yet in thy dark streets shineth the everlasting Light;
The hopes and fears of all the years are met in thee tonight.

For Christ is born of Mary, and gathered all above,
While mortals sleep, the angels keep their watch of
    wond'ring love.
O morning stars, together proclaim the holy birth!
And praises sing to God, the King, and peace to all
    on earth.

How silently, how silently, the wondrous gift is giv'n!
So God imparts to human hearts the blessings of
    his heav'n.
No ear may hear his coming, but in this world of sin,
Where meek souls will receive him, still the dear Christ
    enters in.

O holy Child of Bethlehem, descend to us, we pray;
Cast out our sin and enter in, be born to us today.
We hear the Christmas angels the great glad tidings tell;
O come to us, abide with us, our Lord Emmanuel!

Lyrics: Phillips Brooks, 1867

May the God of hope fill you with all joy and peace as you trust in him, so that you may overflow with hope by the power of the Holy Spirit.

Romans 15:13

Thanks be to God for his indescribable gift!

2 Corinthians 9:15

Hoping does not mean doing nothing. . . . It is the opposite of desperate and panicky manipulations, of scurrying and worrying. And hoping is not dreaming. It is not spinning an illusion or fantasy to protect us from our boredom or our pain. It means a confident, alert expectation that God will do what he said he will do. It is imagination put in the harness of faith. It is a willingness to let God do it his way and in his time.

Eugene H. Peterson, A Long Obedience in the Same Direction

The Christmas message is that there is hope for a ruined humanity—hope of pardon, hope of peace with God, hope of glory—because at the Father's will Jesus became poor and was born in a stable so that thirty years later he might hang on a cross.

J. I. Packer, *Knowing God*

To prepare our hearts for Christmas, we must cultivate the spirit of expectancy.

Handel H. Brown, *Keeping the Spirit of Christmas*

Hope is patience with the lamp lit.

Tertullian

Week 2: Peace

―――― ⊗⊗⊗ ――――

Christ came to bring peace on
earth and goodwill to all.

*J*ust as the ancient Israelites longed for the coming of
the Messiah, who would put all things right, Christians long for the return of Christ our King—the one who will come again in glory. Although Christ's return is a day of promise, it is also a day of judgment (Rom. 14:10–12; 2 Tim. 4:1). As we eagerly anticipate the Second Advent, we pause to consider our readiness for Christ's coming and our need to repent of anything that keeps us from being at peace with God.

Scripture

Psalm 85:1–2, 8–13

Isaiah 40:1–11

2 Peter 3:8–15

Matthew 3:1–12

Questions for Reflection

1. The Scripture selections hold in tension several realities about the coming of Christ:

He will come as both a sovereign Lord *and* a gentle Shepherd (Isa. 40:10–11).

He will come to destroy *and* to build. He will destroy the heavens and the earth, subjecting everything and everyone to judgment; and he will create a new heaven and earth, where righteousness reigns (2 Peter 3:10, 13).

He will come to separate *and* to gather. Just as a farmer sorts wheat from chaff at the harvest, Christ will winnow his harvest, burning the chaff with fire and gathering his wheat into the barn (Matt. 3:12).

His reign will be marked by unfailing love *and* unflinching truth (Ps. 85:10).

- What is your initial response to these pairings that might be considered opposites? Which of these tensions seems hardest to reconcile?

- Of these descriptions which make the most sense to you?
- In what ways have you recently experienced these dual realities in your relationship with Christ? For example, how has Christ been both your sovereign Lord and your gentle Shepherd? How has an experience of judgment (or conviction) also been an experience of renewal? How has unflinching truth also reassured you of his unfailing love?
- How do these divine principles affect your understanding of ways to prepare yourself during this Advent season for Christ's coming?

2. The psalmist wrote, "I listen carefully to what God the LORD is saying, for he speaks peace to his faithful people." And then he gave this warning: "But let them not return to their foolish ways" (Ps. 85:8 NLT).
   - For the psalmist, experiencing peace required listening carefully to what God was saying. Briefly identify the situations or relationships in which you most need peace. What makes it difficult for you to listen carefully to what God might be saying to you in these areas?
   - Peace is also intimately connected to righteousness (Ps. 85:10), faithfulness (Ps. 85:11), and a refusal to fall back into foolish ways (Ps. 85:8). How do these anchors for peace help you experience or better understand God's peace in your life?

3. In chapter 3 Max describes an encounter with a pair of teenage boys that got the better of him. In reflecting on the cause of his uncharacteristic behavior, he writes:

> I'd like to blame my behavior on my state of mind, the stress of the traffic, the driver who nearly hit my car, or the passenger who pushed my buttons. But I can blame my bizarre behavior on only one thing. The punk inside me. For a few minutes at a stoplight near a shopping mall, I forgot who I was.
>
> And I forgot who the teenager was. In that heated moment he wasn't someone's son. He wasn't a creation of God. . . . He was a disrespectful jerk, and I let him bring out the disrespectful jerk in me. (page 26)

- Think of a recent experience in which you realized, *That just wasn't me* or *I just wasn't myself*.
- On what did you want to blame your behavior?
- What did you "forget" about yourself and others?

4. "Under the right circumstances you will do the wrong thing," Max writes. "You won't want to. You'll try not to, but you will. Why? You have a sin nature" (page 26).

- What are your "right circumstances," the conditions in which you are prone to do the wrong thing?
- What three words or phrases best describe you when you are under stress or in your "right circumstances"? How do these characteristics differ from the person you believe you really are, or the person you want to be?

- "Jesus not only did a work *for* us," Max writes, "he does a work *within* us" (pages 29–30). In other words, Jesus not only saves us; he wants to change us. Do you tend to focus more on the fact that Jesus saved you, or the fact that he wants to change you? Why?

5. A central task of Advent, and the Christian life as a whole, is to pursue peace with God—to live today with our eternal tomorrow always in mind. The apostle Peter wrote:

> Since everything will be destroyed in this way, what kind of people ought you to be? You ought to live holy and godly lives as you look forward to the day of God and speed its coming. . . . [S]ince you are looking forward to this, make every effort to be found spotless, blameless and at peace with him. (2 Peter 3:11–12, 14)

We are often caught up in the busyness of *doing*. Time is short, and our to-do lists are long, especially during the holidays. But the invitation of this passage is to focus instead on *being*—specifically, being the kind of people we ought to be.

- How might it change your experience of Advent this year if you were to make your priority *being*—the person you want to become—instead of *doing*?
- When you allow yourself to "look forward to the day of God," what thoughts stir in you? What hopes does it kindle for the kind of person you most want to be?

Advent Prayer
Come, Lord Jesus. You are my peace.

Advent Practice
Consider using one or more of the following options to practice and experience peace this week.

- Make a *being* or a *to-be* list, and keep it with your to-do list. Reread 2 Peter 3:11–14. On the pad of paper or electronic device you typically use to create your daily or weekly to-do list, write down a few phrases or statements that describe the person you hope to be. For example, *I want to be a peacemaker in my relationships*, *I want to be a loving presence*, or *I want to be someone who prioritizes people over projects*. Refer to your to-be list every time you refer to your to-do list—at least once a day—as a way to focus on being at peace with God.
- Set aside a specific time in your calendar this week for self-reflection and confession. In God's loving presence consider the areas where you lack peace with God. It might be habits of thought or behavior, relationships, or circumstances. With specificity acknowledge your guilt—what you have done wrong or left undone. Express your regret and sorrow, asking for God's strength to make things right, to apologize, or to make restitution where appropriate and to keep you from repeating these failures

in the future. Receive God's forgiveness and thank him for giving you his peace.

- Do a peace review each day. Just as coaches and athletes sometimes watch game-day videos so they can analyze and improve their skills, imagine you and Jesus are watching a video replay of the previous day. As you reflect on your morning, afternoon, and evening, consider two questions: *In what ways did I experience peace with God and others? In what ways did I fail to experience peace with God and others?* Use a pad of paper or a journal to note your observations. Prayerfully invite Jesus to coach you on how to pursue and experience greater peace with God and others in the day ahead.

Advent Hymn

O COME, O COME, EMMANUEL

O come, O come, Emmanuel,
And ransom captive Israel,
That mourns in lonely exile here
Until the Son of God appear.
Rejoice! Rejoice!
Emmanuel shall come to thee, O Israel.

O come, Thou Wisdom from on high,
Who orderest all things mightily;
To us the path of knowledge show,
And teach us in her ways to go.
Rejoice! Rejoice!
Emmanuel shall come to thee, O Israel.

O come, Thou Rod of Jesse, free
Thine own from Satan's tyranny;
From depths of hell Thy people save,
And give them victory over the grave.
Rejoice! Rejoice!
Emmanuel shall come to thee, O Israel.

O come, Thou Day-spring, come and cheer
Our spirits by Thine advent here;
Disperse the gloomy clouds of night,

And death's dark shadows put to flight.
Rejoice! Rejoice!
Emmanuel shall come to thee, O Israel.

O come, Thou Key of David, come,
And open wide our heavenly home;
Make safe the way that leads on high,
And close the path to misery.
Rejoice! Rejoice!
Emmanuel shall come to thee, O Israel.

O come, O come, great Lord of might,
Who to Thy tribes on Sinai's height
In ancient times once gave the law
In cloud and majesty and awe.
Rejoice! Rejoice!
Emmanuel shall come to thee, O Israel.

O come, Thou Root of Jesse's tree,
An ensign of Thy people be;
Before Thee rulers silent fall;
All peoples on Thy mercy call.
Rejoice! Rejoice!
Emmanuel shall come to thee, O Israel.

O come, Desire of nations, bind
In one the hearts of all mankind;

Bid Thou our sad divisions cease,
And be Thyself our King of Peace.
Rejoice! Rejoice!
Emmanuel shall come to thee, O Israel.

Lyrics: Traditional Hymn,
translated by John M. Neale, 1851

For a child is born to us, a son is given to us. . . . And
he will be called: Wonderful Counselor, Mighty God,
Everlasting Father, Prince of Peace.

Isaiah 9:6 NLT

Therefore, since we have been made right in God's sight
by faith, we have peace with God because of what Jesus
Christ our Lord has done for us. . . . and we confidently
and joyfully look forward to sharing God's glory.

Romans 5:1–2 NLT

God blesses those who work for peace, for they will be
called the children of God.

Matthew 5:9 NLT

Then Jesus said to her, "Your sins are forgiven. . . . go in peace."

Luke 7:48, 50

Peace [is] the rest of will that results from assurance about how things will turn out.

Dallas Willard, "Willard Words," dwillard.org

It is he who made us and not we ourselves, made us out of his peace to live in peace, out of his light to dwell in light, out of his love to be above all things loved and loving.

Frederick Buechner, *Secrets in the Dark*

Week 3: Joy

Let there be jubilation,
celebration, and festivity!

Our hope is sure, we have peace with God, and the Messiah is coming to set everything right in our sin-drenched world. Every tear will be dried, every hurting heart mended, every broken body healed, every torn relationship restored. We are treasured sons and daughters of the Most High God. The only reasonable response to God's lavish love and goodness is joy—pure joy!

Scripture
Psalm 126
Isaiah 61:1–4, 7–11
1 Thessalonians 5:16–24
Matthew 11:2–11

Questions for Reflection

1. Even when describing joy, the biblical writers never gloss over evil and suffering. The selected passages acknowledge a wide range of dark realities and conditions, among them:

Tears	Imprisonment	Every kind of evil
Weeping	Ashes	Blindness
Mourning	Ruins	Lameness
Grief	Devastations	Deafness
Poverty	Disgrace	Leprosy
Despair	Robbery	Death
Captivity	Wrongdoing	

Max described such unwelcome intrusions in our lives as "interruptions." And the impact? "They can stir fear and anxiety," he writes, "They steal our sleep and pickpocket our joy. They can cause us to question God, even turn away from God" (pages 35–36).

- Which words or phrases on the list come closest to describing a recent "interruption" you've experienced or one you're experiencing now?

- How has this interruption affected you? For example, consider the emotional, physical, relational, and financial consequences.
- Max characterizes Christmas as "a season of interruptions." In what ways, if any, does the holiday season complicate or intensify the effect of your interruptions? In what ways, if any, do the holidays lighten your burden?
- How would you describe your awareness and experience of God throughout this season? For example, does God seem especially close or distant? Do you find yourself turning toward God or away from him, or do you vacillate?

2. The psalmist used the images of seeds and harvest to describe the miracle of God gleaning joy from suffering (Ps. 126:5–6). Author and pastor Eugene Peterson summarized it this way: "All suffering, all pain, all emptiness, all disappointment is seed: sow it in God and he will, finally, bring a crop of joy from it."[1] It is the same resurrection truth the apostle Paul described in his first letter to the church at Corinth:

What is sown is perishable, what is raised is imperishable. It is sown in dishonor, it is raised in glory. It is sown in weakness, it is raised in power. (1 Cor. 15:42–43 NRSV)

If we think of the hardships of this life as seeds, we have at least three options for what we do with them:

We can refuse to plant. We can cling to our hardships and to our lives as they are.

We can plant in God. We can surrender our hardships and our lives in faith, trusting that God can and will produce crops of joy and new life.

We can plant in something other than God. We can choose the shallow soil of distractions or self-defeating behaviors in hopes they will produce a crop of quick relief. As Max acknowledges, "We shop till we drop, drink till we can't think, work till we can't stop" (page 123).

- How do you relate to each of the three options? Which one best describes how you dealt with or are dealing with the situation(s) you identified in question 1?

- Max points us to Psalm 11:3 and an ancient question that echoes today: "When all that is good falls apart, what can good people do?" (NCV). What is falling apart in our world today? What is falling apart in your personal world? Enumerate some of the challenges facing humanity. What interruptions are threatening your personal peace? Answer Max's question: "What is the godly response to these unexpected mishaps and calamities of life?"

God has made a business of turning tragedy into triumph. In what ways do the lives of Joseph, Moses, Daniel, and Jesus challenge and encourage you? How can your own encounter with adversity move you closer to understanding the sufferings of Christ?

3. The psalmist rehearsed God's wonders from the *past* and concluded, "Yes, the LORD has done amazing things for us! What joy!" (Ps. 126:3 NLT). When the prophet Isaiah considered how God had already saved him and also looked forward to what God would do in the *future*, he responded, "I am overwhelmed with joy in the LORD my God!" (Isa. 61:10 NLT). When it came to joy, the apostle Paul said there is no time like the *present*: "Always be joyful" (1 Thess. 5:16 NLT). Joy is a time traveler. It constantly scans the timeline—from ancient history to infinity—and sets up camp on every occasion and every promise of God's lavish goodness.

- What brings you the greatest joy—remembering the past, experiencing the present, or anticipating the future? Which brings the least joy?

- Advent is a time-traveling season. There is joy in remembering God's gift of the Christ child, joy in celebrating God's presence with us now, and joy in anticipating the Second Advent. Which of these three sources of joy resonates most with you this Advent? Why?

Advent Prayer
Come, Lord Jesus. Be my joy.

Advent Practice
Consider using one or more of the following options to practice and experience joy this week.

- Plant a seed as an expression of trust that just as God will bring a plant from that seed, he will also bring a crop of joy from the seeds of every hardship you sow in him. For example, the bulbs of amaryllis flowers are often used as gifts during the Christmas season. The bulbs are typically sold in pots, grow well indoors, and need just a bit of sun and water to grow and bloom. But any seed will do, even grass seed! Follow the directions for planting and growing your seed(s) indoors, and allow the process of sowing, waiting, and growth to be a touchstone for your own reflections and growth in joy.
- Engage in "time travel" to search for joy. Use your journal or a notepad to create a three-column chart. At the top of the columns, write *Past*, *Present*, and *Future*. In each column write at least two or three ways in which you recognize God's lavish goodness to you—actions he has taken on your behalf. Then write down in each column any questions you have for God or any ways you are struggling to recognize God's goodness to you in that time period. Close with prayer, offering your chart

to God. Express your joy for his goodness to you and entrust your questions to him, asking to see the light of his goodness even in the dark places.

- As you reflect on the "interruption" of Jenna's miscarriage, ask God to remind you of a young couple experiencing a similar season of sadness. Pray for them, and ask God to show you how you might comfort and encourage them in the days ahead.

Advent Hymn

GOD REST YE MERRY, GENTLEMEN

God rest ye merry, gentlemen,
Let nothing you dismay,
Remember Christ our Savior
Was born on Christmas Day;
To save us all from Satan's power
When we were gone astray.
O tidings of comfort and joy, comfort and joy;
O tidings of comfort and joy.

In Bethlehem, in Israel,
This blessèd Babe was born,
And laid within a manger
Upon this blessèd morn;
The which His mother Mary
Did nothing take in scorn.
O tidings of comfort and joy, comfort and joy;
O tidings of comfort and joy.

From God our heavenly Father
A blessèd angel came;
And unto certain shepherds
Brought tidings of the same;
How that in Bethlehem was born
The Son of God by name.

O tidings of comfort and joy, comfort and joy;
O tidings of comfort and joy.

Fear not, then, said the angel,
Let nothing you affright
This day is born a Savior
Of a pure Virgin bright,
To free all those who trust in Him
From Satan's power and might.
O tidings of comfort and joy, comfort and joy;
O tidings of comfort and joy.

The shepherds at those tidings
Rejoiced much in mind,
And left their flocks a-feeding
In tempest, storm and wind,
And went to Bethl'em straightaway
This blessèd Babe to find.
O tidings of comfort and joy, comfort and joy;
O tidings of comfort and joy.

Now to the Lord sing praises
All you within this place,
And with true love and brotherhood
Each other now embrace;
This holy tide of Christmas
All others doth deface.

O tidings of comfort and joy, comfort and joy;
O tidings of comfort and joy.

Lyrics: Traditional English Carol

You thrill me, LORD, with all you have done for me! I sing for joy because of what you have done.

Psalm 92:4 NLT

You make known to me the path of life; you will fill me with joy in your presence, with eternal pleasures at your right hand.

Psalm 16:11

The joy of the LORD is your strength.

Nehemiah 8:10

Joy has a history. Joy is the verified, repeated experience of those involved in what God is doing.

Eugene H. Peterson, *A Long Obedience in the Same Direction*

———∞∞∞———

Joy is nurtured by anticipation. . . . Just as joy builds on the past, it borrows from the future. It expects certain things to happen.

Eugene H. Peterson, *A Long Obedience in the Same Direction*

———∞∞∞———

True joy, happiness, and inner peace come from the giving of ourselves to others. A happy life is a life for others.

Henri J. M. Nouwen, *Life of the Beloved*

Week 4: Love

It really comes down to that:
God loves us.

"First we were loved," wrote the apostle John, "now we love" (1 John 4:19 MSG). God always takes the initiative—he blessed first, served first, comforted first, and most of all, loved first. And then it's up to us. How will we respond? At Advent, while much of the world around us is enamored by distractions and lesser loves, we seek to discover anew our first love, the love that "came down at Christmas,"[2] and then to share that love by blessing, serving, and comforting others.

Scripture

Psalm 89:1–4, 19–26
Micah 5:2–5a
Titus 3:3–8
Luke 1:39–55

Questions for Reflection

1. "The story of Christmas is the story of God's relentless love for us," Max writes, "Let him love you. . . . You might question his actions, decisions, or declarations. But you can never, ever question his zany, stunning, unquenchable affection" (pages 134–135).

   • As you reflect on your relationship with God, when would you say you were most aware and most certain of God's love for you? How, specifically, did you let God love you?

   • Even though God's love is always apparent, we go through seasons when we doubt it. What, if anything, has led you to question God's love for you?

   • Do you find it difficult to let God love you in your current season of life? Why or why not?

2. When it came to expressing the wonder of God's love, the psalmist couldn't help but break into song:

   I will sing of the LORD's great love forever;
       with my mouth I will make your faithfulness known
       through all generations.

I will declare that your love stands firm forever,
> that you have established your faithfulness in heaven
> itself. (Ps. 89:1–2)

This is a heart-wide-open declaration that reflects all the fervency and devotion of a first love. The psalmist essentially said to God, "Your loyal love is so amazing that I will never stop singing about it!"

- Using temperature as a gauge, which of the following statements comes closest to describing your heart right now?
  - *Hot.* I am so amazed by God's love for me I can't help sharing it with others.
  - *Warm.* I am committed to my faith, but I'm not as passionate about God or as loving toward others as I should be.
  - *Cold.* I feel distant from or ambivalent about God.
  - *Other:*
- What connections could you make between the statement you just checked and your responses to question 1? In other words, how might your willingness to let God love you affect your ability to love God and others wholeheartedly?

3. The apostle Paul sought to rekindle in his readers the flames of love for God and others by reminding them about who they were before they received God's love:

We . . . were foolish, disobedient, deceived and enslaved
by all kinds of passions and pleasures. We lived in
malice and envy, being hated and hating one another.
But when the kindness and love of God our Savior
appeared, he saved us, not because of righteous things
we had done, but because of his mercy. (Titus 3:3–5)

Jesus said, "A person who is forgiven little shows only
little love" (Luke 7:47 NLT). Paul wanted his readers to
show great love, so he reminded them of how much they
had been forgiven. He then spelled out the implications
of God's sacrificial love for us:

I want you to stress these things, so that those
who have trusted in God may be careful to devote
themselves to doing what is good. (Titus 3:8)

- What words or phrases come to mind when you
  consider who you were before you gave your life to
  Christ and received God's love? (If you find this difficult
  because you gave your life to Christ as a child, use
  the apostle Paul's description as a starting point and
  consider instead the darkness you were saved from
  because of your early relationship with God.)
- How does remembering who you were before Christ
  (or what Christ has saved you from) affect you? In
  what ways, if any, does it increase your awareness of
  your love for Christ?

4. Echoing the apostle Paul's teaching in the Titus passage, Max writes, "In the manger God loves you; through the cross God saves you. But has he taken you to his home? Not yet. He has work for you to do. He wants the world to see what God can do with his purchased possessions" (page 125).

- It has been said, "It is Christmas every time you let God love others through you." How have you recently experienced "Christmas" because God loved you through someone else?

- What words or phrases would characterize this person and his or her devotion to doing what is good (Titus 3:8)? Based on his or her example, how would you complete the following sentence in your own words? *Letting God love others through me means . . .*

- How would you describe the work that you sense God has for you to do right now, the ways in which he seems to be inviting you to do good and bring "Christmas" to others? Or, what do you hope God can do with you, his beloved possession?

Advent Prayer
Come, Lord Jesus. I love you.

Advent Practice
Consider using one or more of the following options to practice giving and receiving love this week.

- Focus your thoughts and daily prayers on your love relationship with God. At the beginning of each day, invite God to show you how he loves you. Drawing on the example of Psalm 89, tell God how much you love him, focusing not only on his good gifts to you but also on who he is—loving, patient, good, holy. Or if you struggle to express your love to God, tell him why, and ask for his help. Before the week is done, "go public," as the psalmist did, and share with at least one other person something you've learned about God's love for you or your love for God or an example of how God demonstrated his love for you this week. If you find it helpful, write down your daily prayers, your expressions of love to God, and your observations as you look expectantly each day for God to show you how he loves you.

- Author Glennon Doyle Melton wrote, "Every time we open our mouths and speak, we are either saying *let there be light* or *let there be darkness*."[3] In the spirit of Advent, show love this week by seeking to bring light with every word you speak. As a visual reminder, use the image of a star or a candle as the wallpaper on your laptop or phone, or place a few sticky notes around your home or workplace that say, "Speak light!" or "Let there be light!"

- Choose one relationship to focus on this week. It might be a spouse, a child, a parent, a coworker, a friend. Filter every interaction with this person through one question: What does love require of me in this moment? Then do it. Let love dictate your demeanor, your body language, your words, your actions. Use a notepad or a journal to write down your observations each day, recording any challenges or effect your commitment to love has on your relationship.

Advent Hymn

ANGELS FROM THE REALMS OF GLORY

Angels from the realms of glory,
Wing your flight o'er all the earth;
Ye who sang creation's story
Now proclaim Messiah's birth.
Come and worship, come and worship,
Worship Christ, the newborn king.

Shepherds, in the field abiding,
Watching o'er your flocks by night,
God with us is now residing;
Yonder shines the infant light:
Come and worship, come and worship,
Worship Christ, the newborn king.

Sages, leave your contemplations,
Brighter visions beam afar;
Seek the great Desire of nations;
Ye have seen His natal star.
Come and worship, come and worship,
Worship Christ, the newborn king.

Saints, before the altar bending,
Watching long in hope and fear;
Suddenly the Lord, descending,

In His temple shall appear.
Come and worship, come and worship,
Worship Christ, the newborn king.

Sinners, wrung with true repentance,
Doomed for guilt to endless pains,
Justice now revokes the sentence,
Mercy calls you; break your chains.
Come and worship, come and worship,
Worship Christ, the newborn king.

Though an Infant now we view Him,
He shall fill His Father's throne,
Gather all the nations to Him;
Every knee shall then bow down:
Come and worship, come and worship,
Worship Christ, the newborn king.

All creation, join in praising
God, the Father, Spirit, Son,
Evermore your voices raising
To th'eternal Three in One.
Come and worship, come and worship,
Worship Christ, the newborn king.

Lyrics: James Montgomery, 1816

See what great love the Father has lavished on us, that we should be called children of God! And that is what we are!

1 John 3:1

Regardless of what else you put on, wear love. It's your basic, all-purpose garment. Never be without it.

Colossians 3:14 MSG

[Jesus] does not call us to do what he did, but to be as he was, permeated with love. Then the doing of what he did and said becomes the natural expression of who we are in him.

Dallas Willard, *The Divine Conspiracy*

The heavenly Father cherishes the earth and each human being upon it. The fondness, the endearment, the unstintingly affectionate regard of God toward all his creatures is the natural outflow of what he is to the core—which we vainly try to capture with our tired but indispensable old word "love."

Dallas Willard, *The Divine Conspiracy*

———— ∞∞∞ ————

Truly he taught us to love one another, his law is love and his gospel is peace.

Placide Cappeau, "O Holy Night"

———— ∞∞∞ ————

Turn around and believe that the good news that we are loved is gooder than we ever dared hope, and that to believe in that good news, to live out of it and toward it, to be in love with that good news, is of all glad things in this world the gladdest thing of all.

Amen, and come, Lord Jesus.

Frederick Buechner, *The Clown in the Belfry*

Christmas Eve / Christmas Day

God became one of us so we could
become one with him.

*T*he joy and promise of Christmas is that the miracle of
Bethlehem still happens. God still enters into the reality
of our messy everyday lives and loves us. And so on this day,
we open wide our hearts to receive the Christ child with joy.

Scripture
Psalm 96
Isaiah 9:2–7
Hebrews 1:1–12
Luke 2:1–20

Questions for Reflection

1. Luke's account of Jesus' birth includes several characters and lots of action:

   Mary and Joseph undertake a long journey under adverse conditions.

   The Christ child is born in a humble stable.

   The angel of the Lord brings good news of great joy to the shepherds.

   The heavenly host praises God.

   The shepherds are initially afraid but then receive and share the good news.

   All who hear the good news are amazed.

   Mary treasures up and ponders all she has experienced.

   - As you read the passage from Luke 2, which characters or circumstances best represent you in your relationship with Jesus right now? For example, like Mary and Joseph, perhaps you find yourself in the midst of a difficult journey with Christ, seeking shelter and rest. Like the Christ child, you may be in humble or vulnerable circumstances, longing for comfort and care.

   - How does the character or circumstance you identified help you understand what you long for in your relationship with Christ?

2. Luke pointed out a compelling contrast when he noted that "all who heard it were *amazed*. . . . But Mary *treasured up* all these things and *pondered* them in her heart" (Luke 2:18–19, emphasis mine).

- To be amazed is to be astonished, surprised, or stunned. Depending on the circumstances, amazement might lead to admiration and wonder, or to shock and bewilderment. The contrast Luke identified between Mary and "all who . . . were amazed" doesn't suggest that Mary's response was better, but it was noticeably different. Based on your own experiences, how would you describe the difference between the two responses? What changes in you when you move from being amazed at an experience to treasuring or pondering that experience?

- The Greek words translated "treasured up" and "pondered," mean to keep safe and close, to protect and preserve in memory, to bring together in one's mind or to confer with oneself. During the four weeks of Advent, you've had a chance to reflect on many truths about the gifts we receive from Christ—hope, peace, joy, and love. As you reflect on this four-week journey, what insights or experiences—with God and others—do you want to treasure up? Briefly identify a few, and then allow yourself to ponder them in God's presence, thanking him for these gifts and inviting him to reveal to you something of himself through them.

3. Max writes, "If the King was willing to enter the world of animals and shepherds and swaddling clothes, don't you think he's willing to enter yours? He took on your face in the hope that you would see his" (page 20).

- As you anticipate not only your celebration of Christmas but also the days and weeks to come, in what circumstance or relationship do you feel the greatest need to see the face of Immanuel, God with you?
- "When Christ was born, so was our hope. . . . The manger . . . dares us to believe the best is yet to be. And it could all begin today" (page 135, 9). What is the best you might dare to believe about the circumstance or relationship you just identified? Prayerfully surrender these hopes to God, trusting that he is already at work to provide the light you seek, the help you need, the deliverance you long for.

Christmas Prayer
Welcome, Lord Jesus. Make my heart your home this day.

Christmas Practice
God created celebration: he is the author of joy, pleasure, and merriment. In fact, Jesus described the kingdom as a great banquet to which everyone is invited (Matt. 22:1–14). At Christmas we train our hearts for heaven by celebrating God's miraculous gift of Jesus. And just as Paul and Silas chose to sing praises even while imprisoned (Acts 16:22–25), we can choose joy and celebration at Christmas regardless of our circumstances. Author and pastor Adele Calhoun wrote:

The world is filled with reasons to be downcast. But deeper than sorrow thrums the unbroken pulse of God's joy, a joy that will yet have its eternal day. To set our hearts on this joy reminds us that we can choose how we respond to any particular moment. We can search for God in all circumstances, or not. We can seek the pulse of hope and celebration because it is God's reality. Heaven is celebrating. . . . Every small experience of Jesus with us is a taste of the joy that is to come. We are not alone—and that in itself is reason to celebrate.[4]

God invites you to choose joy this day, to follow the happy commands of the psalmist: *Sing! Praise! Proclaim! Declare! Worship!* (see Psalm 96). Max puts it this way:

For your own sake do what the angels did: make a big deal about the arrival of the King. . . . Do you love God? Let him know. Tell him! Out loud. In public. Unashamed. Let there be jubilation, celebration, and festivity! (page 65–66)

And you can choose joy in quiet ways as well. Be watchful for "every small experience of Jesus," knowing that he often shows up in unexpected ways. Treasure up and ponder all the ways Christ reveals himself to you—in events, music, meals, relationships, beauty, and the comfort of his presence with you.

Christmas Hymn

HARK! THE HERALD ANGELS SING

Hark! The herald angels sing,
Glory to the newborn King;
Peace on earth, and mercy mild,
God and sinners reconciled!

Joyful, all ye nations rise,
Join the triumph of the skies;
Nature rise and worship him,
Who is born in Bethlehem!

Christ, by highest Heav'n adored;
Christ the everlasting Lord;
Late in time, behold Him come,
Offspring of a virgin's womb.

Veiled in flesh the Godhead see;
Hail th'incarnate Deity,
Pleas'd as Man with Men t'appear,
Jesus our Emmanuel here.

Hail the Heav'n-born Prince of Peace
Hail the Son of Righteousness!
Light and Life around he brings,
Ris'n with Healing in his Wings.

Mild he lays his Glory by,
Born that Men no more may die;
Born to raise the Sons of Earth,
Born to give them second Birth.

> Lyrics: Charles Wesley (1739) and George Whitefield (1753)

— ∞∞ —

The Word became flesh and blood, and moved into the neighborhood.

> John 1:14 MSG

— ∞∞ —

I bring you good news that will bring great joy to all people. The Savior—yes, the Messiah, the Lord—has been born today in Bethlehem, the city of David!

> Luke 2:10–11 NLT

— ∞∞ —

For this is how God loved the world: He gave his one and only Son, so that everyone who believes in him will not perish but have eternal life.

> John 3:16 NLT

— ∞∞ —

You always get your Christmas miracle. You get God with you. . . .

Christ is all your good, and He is all yours, and this is always all your miracle.

No matter the barrenness you feel, you can always have as much of Jesus as you want.

Ann Voskamp, *The Greatest Gift*

The eternal Son became a child so that I might become a child again and so reenter with him into the Kingdom of the Father.

Henri J. M. Nouwen, *The Return of the Prodigal Son*

Who can add to Christmas? The perfect motive is that God so loved the world.

The perfect gift is that he gave his only Son.

The only requirement is to believe in him.

The reward of faith is that you shall have everlasting life.

attributed to Corrie ten Boom

Notes

Chapter 2: God Has a Face
1. Max Lucado, *God Came Near: Chronicles of the Christ* (Portland, OR: Multnomah, 1987).
2. John 11:1–36; Matthew 14:22–33; John 8:1–11.
3. Stephen Seamands, *Give Them Christ: Preaching His Incarnation, Crucifixion, Resurrection, Ascension and Return* (Downers Grove, IL: IVP Books, 2012), 38–40.

Chapter 3: Saved from Ourselves
1. Frederick Dale Bruner, *Matthew: A Commentary,* vol. 1, *The Christbook: Matthew 1–12,* rev. and exp. ed. (Grand Rapids: William B. Eerdmans, 2004), 29–30.

Chapter 6: Worship Works Wonders
1. Terry Wardle, *Exalt Him! Designing Dynamic Worship Services* (Camp Hill, PA: Christian Publications, 1992), 23.
2. "Always on My Mind," by Wayne Carson, Johnny Christopher, and Mark James, published 1972.

3. Matthew 12:34 NKJV.

4. John Wesley, *The Works of the Reverend John Wesley, A. M.* (New York: B. Waugh and T. Mason, 1835), 7:609.

5. Harold Boulton, "All Through the Night," http://www. carols.org.uk/a45-all-through-the-night.htm.

6. "Bertie Felstead," *The Economist*, August 2, 2001, http:// www.economist.com/node/718781.

Chapter 7: God Guides the Wise

1. Frederick Dale Bruner, *Matthew: A Commentary*, vol. 1, *The Christbook: Matthew 1–12*, rev. and exp. ed. (Grand Rapids: William B. Eerdmans, 2004), 60.

2. "Water Scene," *The Miracle Worker*, directed by Paul Aaron (1979; Atlanta, GA: Half-Pint Productions).

Chapter 8: Humility Shines

1. Dean Farrar, *The Life of Christ* (London: Cassell, n.d.), 22–23.

2. Flavius Josephus, *The Works of Josephus*, updated ed., trans. William Whiston (Peabody, MA: Hendrickson, 1987), 882.

3. G. K. Chesterton, *Orthodoxy* (Hollywood, FL: Simon and Brown, 2012), 17.

4. *The International Standard Bible Encyclopedia*, ed., Geoffrey W. Bromiley, vol. 2, *E–J* (Grand Rapids: William B. Eerdmans, 1982), 693.

Chapter 9: Perhaps Today

1. Norval Geldenhuys, *Commentary on the Gospel of Luke: The English Text with Introduction, Exposition and Notes* (Grand Rapids: William B. Eerdmans, 1954), 117–18.

2. Dean Farrar, *The Life of Christ* (London: Cassell, n.d.), 40.

3. Walter L. Liefeld, "Luke," in *The Expositor's Bible Commentary*, ed. Frank E. Gaebelein (Grand Rapids: Zondervan, 1984), 8:849.

4. Edmund Sears, "That Glorious Song of Old," v. 2, public domain.

Chapter 10: Crown, Cradle, and Cross

1. "Whirlpool Galaxy Facts," Space Facts, http://space-facts. com/whirlpool-galaxy/.

2. Tim Sharp, "How Big Is the Sun?/Size of the Sun," Space. com, August 8, 2012, www.space.com/17001-how-big-is-the-sun-size-of-the-sun.html.

3. Space.com staff, "Supergiant Star's Rainbow Nebula Revealed," Space.com, June 23, 2011, http://www.space. com/12051-bright-nebula-photo-supergiant-star-betelgeuse. html.

4. Miriam Kramer, "Supergiant Star Betelgeuse to Crash into Cosmic 'Wall,'" Space.com, January 25, 2013, http://www. space.com/19415-supergiant-star-betelgeuse-crash-photo. html.

5. Extract by C S Lewis © copyright C S Lewis Pte Ltd. Used by permission.

Chapter 11: It's Good-Bye to the Bents

1. Rick Warren, *The Purpose of Christmas* (New York: Howard Books, 2008), 41.

2. John 4:4–29.

3. Mark 5:1–15.

4. Luke 19:1–10.

Chapter 12: Every Day a Christmas, Every Heart a Manger

1. Joseph F. Kelly, *The Birth of Christmas* (Waco, TX: Center for Christian Ethics at Baylor University, 2011), 15, http://www.baylor.edu/content/services/document.php/159119.pdf.
2. J. B. Phillips, *New Testament Christianity* (Eugene, OR: Wipf and Stock, 2012), 15–16.

Study Guide Sessions

1. Eugene H. Peterson, *A Long Obedience in the Same Direction: Discipleship in an Instant Society*, rev. and exp. ed. (Downer's Grove, IL: InterVarsity Press, 1980, 2000), 100.
2. Christina Rossetti, "Love Came Down at Christmas," All Poetry, http://allpoetry.com/Love-Came-Down-at-Christmas.
3. Glennon Doyle Melton, https://www.facebook.com/glennondoylemelton, Facebook post, April 12, 2015.
4. Adele Ahlberg Calhoun, *Spiritual Disciplines Handbook: Practices That Transform Us* (Downers Grove, IL: InterVarsity Press, 2005), 27.

❧ The Lucado Reader's Guide ❧

Discover . . . Inside every book by Max Lucado, you'll find words of
encouragement and inspiration that will draw you into a deeper experience with
Jesus and treasures for your walk with God. What will you discover?

3:16: The Numbers of Hope
. . . the 26 words that can change
your life.
core scripture: John 3:16

And the Angels Were Silent
. . . what Jesus Christ's final days can
teach you about what matters most.
core scripture: Matthew 20–27

The Applause of Heaven
. . . the secret to a truly satisfying life.
core scripture: The Beatitudes,
Matthew 5:1–10

Before Amen
. . . the power of a simple prayer.
core scripture: Psalm 145:19

Come Thirsty
how to rehydrate your heart
and sink into the wellspring of
God's love.
core scripture: John 7:37–38

Cure for the Common Life
. . . the unique things God designed
you to do with your life.
core scripture: 1 Corinthians 12:7

Facing Your Giants
. . . when God is for you,
no challenge is too great.
core scripture: 1 and 2 Samuel

Fearless
. . . how faith is the antidote to
the fear in your life.
core scripture: John 14:1, 3

A Gentle Thunder
. . . the God who will do whatever it
takes to lead his children back to him.
core scripture: Psalm 81:7

Glory Days
. . . how you fight from victory, not
for it.
core scripture: Joshua 21:43–45

God Came Near
. . . a love so great that it left heaven
to become part of your world.
core scripture: John 1:14

Grace
. . . the incredible gift that saves
and sustains you.
core scripture: Hebrews 12:15

Great Day, Every Day
. . . how living in a purposeful way
will help you trust more, stress less.
core scripture: Psalm 118:24

The Great House of God
. . . a blueprint for peace, joy, and
love found in the Lord's Prayer.
core scripture: The Lord's Prayer,
Matthew 6:9–13

He Chose the Nails
. . . a love so deep that it chose death
on a cross—just to win your heart.
core scripture: 1 Peter 1:18–20

He Still Moves Stones
. . . the God who still does the
impossible—in your life.
core scripture: Matthew 12:20

In the Eye of the Storm
. . . peace in the storms of your life.
core scripture: John 6

In the Grip of Grace
. . . the greatest gift of all—the
grace of God.
core scripture: Romans

It's Not About Me
. . . why focusing on God will make
sense of your life.
core scripture: 2 Corinthians 3:18

Just Like Jesus
. . . a life free from guilt, fear,
and anxiety.
core scripture: Ephesians 4:23–24

A Love Worth Giving
. . . how living loved frees you
to love others.
core scripture: 1 Corinthians 13

Next Door Savior
. . . a God who walked life's
hardest trials—and still walks
with you through yours.
core scripture: Matthew 16:13–16

No Wonder They Call Him
the Savior
. . . hope in the unlikeliest place—
upon the cross.
core scripture: Romans 5:15

Outlive Your Life
. . . that a great God created you
to do great things.
core scripture: Acts 1

Six Hours One Friday
. . . forgiveness and healing in
the middle of loss and failure.
core scripture: John 19–20

Traveling Light
. . . the power to release the burdens
you were never meant to carry.
core scripture: Psalm 23

When God Whispers
Your Name
. . . the path to hope in knowing that
God knows you, never forgets you, and
cares about the details of your life.
core scripture: John 10:3

When Christ Comes
. . . why the best is yet to come.
core scripture: 1 Corinthians 15:23

You'll Get Through This
. . . hope in the midst of your hard
times and a God who uses the mess
of life for good.
core scripture: Genesis 50:20

Recommended reading if you're struggling with . . .

FEAR AND WORRY

Before Amen
Come Thirsty
Fearless
For the Tough Times
Next Door Savior
Traveling Light

DISCOURAGEMENT

He Still Moves Stones
Next Door Savior

GRIEF/DEATH OF A LOVED ONE

Next Door Savior
Traveling Light
When Christ Comes
When God Whispers Your Name
You'll Get Through This

GUILT

In the Grip of Grace
Just Like Jesus

LONELINESS

God Came Near

SIN

Before Amen
Facing Your Giants
He Chose the Nails
Six Hours One Friday

WEARINESS

Before Amen
When God Whispers Your Name
You'll Get Through This

Recommended reading if you want to know more about . . .

THE CROSS

And the Angels Were Silent
He Chose the Nails
No Wonder They Call Him the Savior
Six Hours One Friday

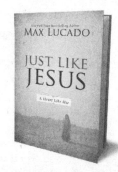

GRACE

Before Amen
Grace
He Chose the Nails
In the Grip of Grace

HEAVEN

The Applause of Heaven
When Christ Comes

SHARING THE GOSPEL

God Came Near
Grace
No Wonder They Call Him the Savior

Recommended reading if you're looking for more . . .

COMFORT

For the Tough Times
He Chose the Nails
Next Door Savior
Traveling Light
You'll Get Through This

COMPASSION

Outlive Your Life

COURAGE

Facing Your Giants
Fearless

HOPE

3:16: The Numbers of Hope
Before Amen
Facing Your Giants
A Gentle Thunder
God Came Near
Grace

JOY

The Applause of Heaven
Cure for the Common Life
When God Whispers Your Name

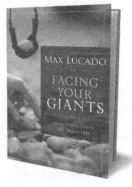

LOVE

Come Thirsty
A Love Worth Giving
No Wonder They Call Him the Savior

PEACE

And the Angels Were Silent
Before Amen
The Great House of God
In the Eye of the Storm
Traveling Light
You'll Get Through This

SATISFACTION

And the Angels Were Silent
Come Thirsty
Cure for the Common Life
Great Day Every Day

TRUST

A Gentle Thunder
It's Not About Me
Next Door Savior

Max Lucado books make great gifts!
If you're coming up to a special occasion, consider one of these.

FOR ADULTS:

For the Tough Times
Grace for the Moment
Live Loved
The Lucado Life Lessons Study Bible
Mocha with Max
DaySpring Daybrighteners® and cards

FOR TEENS/GRADUATES:

Let the Journey Begin
You Can Be Everything God Wants You to Be
You Were Made to Make a Difference

FOR KIDS:

Just in Case You Ever Wonder
The Oak Inside the Acorn
You Are Special

FOR PASTORS AND TEACHERS:

God Thinks You're Wonderful
You Changed My Life

AT CHRISTMAS:

The Crippled Lamb
The Christmas Candle
God Came Near

Tools for your Church and Small Group

Because of Bethlehem/He Chose the Nails: A DVD Study

ISBN: 025986687847

$29.99

Max Lucado leads four video sessions that take small groups through *Because of Bethlehem* and the Advent season, a time of anticipation and celebration. And the story of Easter continues what Christmas began. In five additional sessions, Max unpacks the promises of the cross in *He Chose the Nails*, perfect for the Lenten season.

Because of Bethlehem Study Guide

ISBN: 9780310687054

$9.99

In this four-session video-based study, bestselling author Max Lucado reveals that because of Bethlehem, we have the promise that God is always near us, always for us, and always in us.

Explore the Promises of Christmas in Color

ISBN: 9780718089788

$15.99

Bestselling author Max Lucado invites you to step out of the harried holidays and reconnect with the Christ of Christmas by meditating on the greatest gift ever given. As you add your personal touch to these inspirational Christmastime quotes, you'll discover joy and refreshment in the God who is always near you, always for you, and always in you.

"The King has come! Even for a little one like me."

ISBN: 9780718088873
$8.99

For kids who feel too small or too ordinary comes a Christmas story that reminds us that Christ the King has come for everyone.

Experience Anew the Joy of Christmas

ISBN: 9781401689940

$16.99

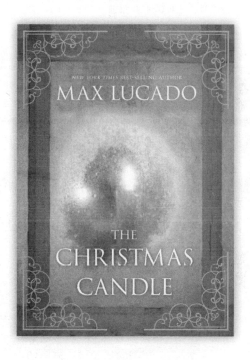

Imagine a Victorian England village in the Cotswolds where very little out of the ordinary ever happens . . . except at Christmas time. This year, Edward Haddington, a lowly candle maker, is visited by a mysterious angel. That angel silently imparts a precious gift—a gift that's bungled and subsequently lost. When the candle maker and his wife finally find the gift, they face a difficult choice. Who among their community is most in need of a Christmas miracle?

Spread the Joy of Christmas

———⊷⊶⊷———

Celebrate the birth of Christ with a DaySpring® *Because of Bethlehem* Advent calendar, Christmas cards, and Christmas tree ornaments. Encourage someone special or treat yourself with these beautiful pieces you'll want to display at this time every year.

DaySpring.com

DaySpring

Christmas Music
from The Salvation Army

New York Staff Band
THE MESSAGE OF CHRISTMAS

1. Selection - The Message of Christmas (William Himes)
2. Intrada - Christmas Intrada (David Rowsell)
3. Christmas Day (Kevin Norbury)
4. Trombone Solo – Room in My Heart, soloist Brett Baker (Michael Kenyon)
5. Coventry Carol (William Broughton)
6. In Heavenly Peace (Terry Camsey)
7. March - Sounds Like Christmas (Norman Bearcroft)
8. The Wexford Carol (Dorothy Gates)
9. Adeste Fidelis (Franz Liszt, arr. Ronald Holz)
10. Christmas Angels (Kenneth Downie)
11. Cornet Solo - O Little Town, soloist Gordon Ward (Ralph Pearce)
12. The Festive Season (Paul Curnow)
13. Away in a Manger (William Broughton)
14. Celebrate the Season (Andrew Blyth)

Carolers' Favorites
133 CHRISTMAS CAROLS AND HOLIDAY SONGS
$ 9.95 Instrumental books
$ 19.95 Vocal/Score book

- Quality 4-part (optional 5th part) arrangements by Erik Leidzen, James Curnow & Stephen Bulla
  - 18 Instrumental books available for Concert Band, Orchestra and Bass Ensemble – Part 1: Bb, Eb, C Part 2: Bb, Eb, C, F Part 3: Bb, Eb, C (Bass clef), F, Alto Clef Part 4: Bb, Eb, C (Bass clef) Part 5: Bb, C (Bass clef) Percussion
  - Vocal and Instrumental books are compatible musically and numerically

Don't miss these stories from Max!

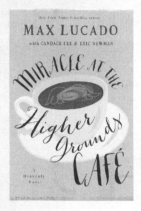

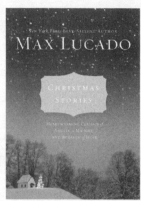

Available in print and e-book!

Inspired by what you just read?
Connect with Max.

Listen to Max's teaching ministry, UpWords, on the radio and online. Visit www.MaxLucado.com to get FREE resources for spiritual growth and encouragement, including:

- Archives of UpWords, Max's daily radio program, and a list of radio stations where it airs
- Devotionals and e-mails from Max
- First look at book excerpts
- Downloads of audio, video, and printed material
- Mobile content

You will also find an online store and special offers.

www.MaxLucado.com

1-800-822-9673

UpWords Ministries
P.O. Box 692170
San Antonio, TX 78269-2170

Join the Max Lucado community:

Follow Max on Twitter @MaxLucado
or at Facebook.com/MaxLucado